"The point in history at which we stand is full of promise and danger. The world will either move forward toward unity and shared prosperity - or it will move apart."

FRANKLIN D. ROOSEVELT
US President

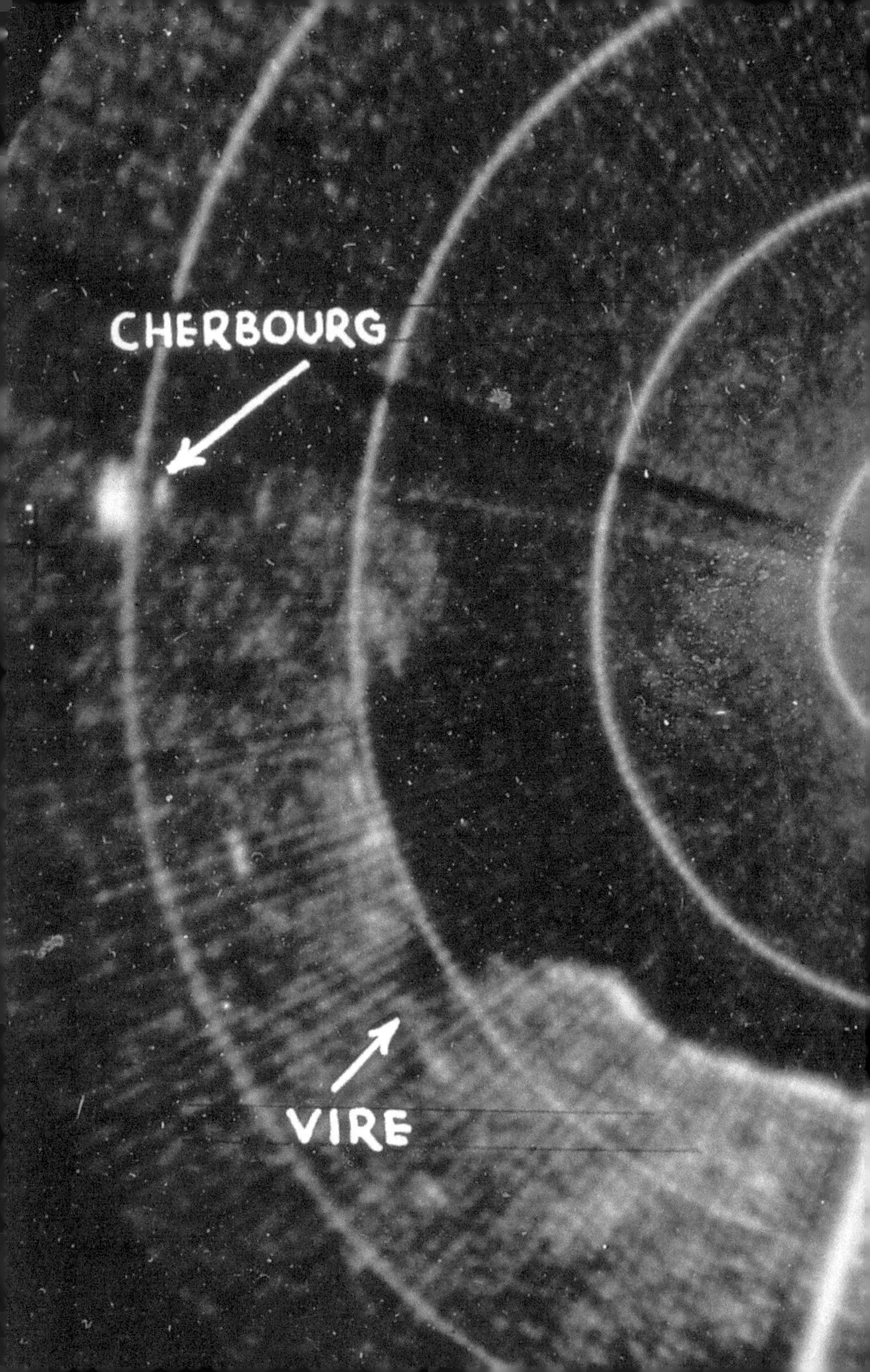
CHERBOURG
VIRE

How do you navigate the ever-changing landscape of life to see beyond current circumstances and be free to create your future history today?

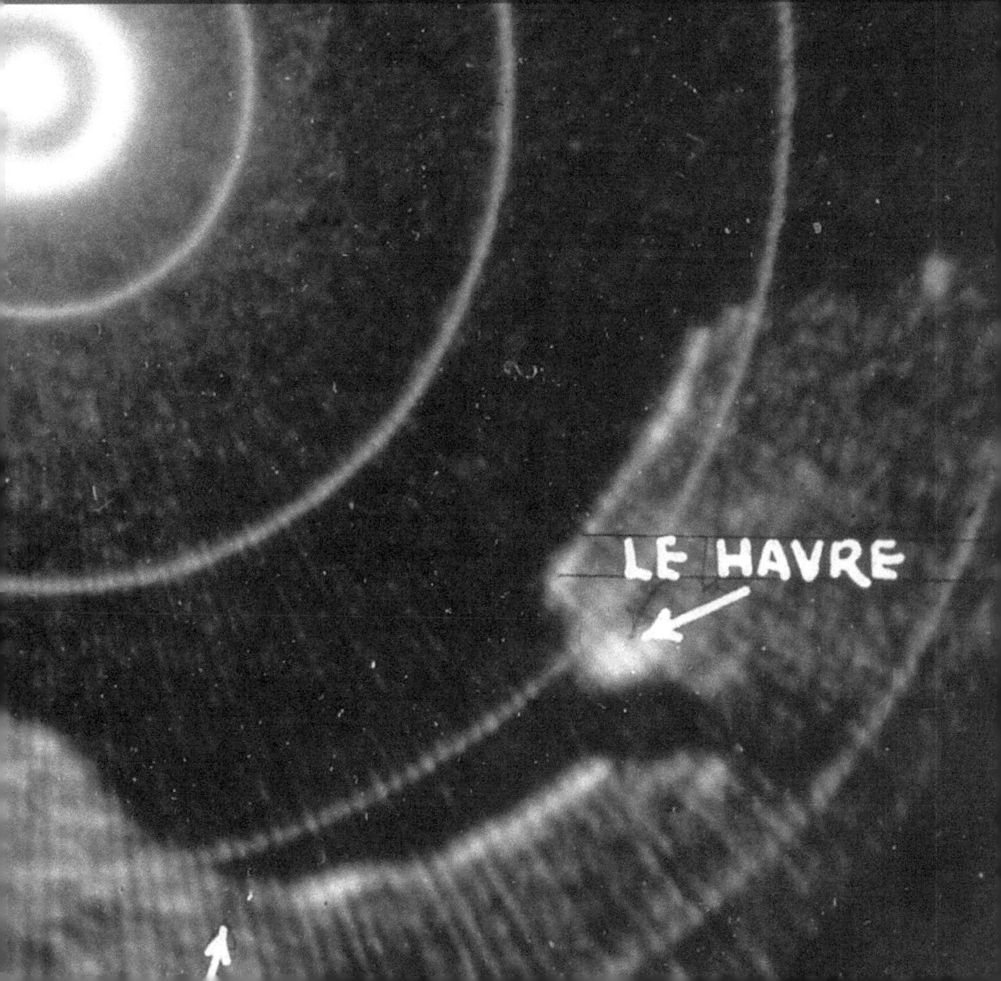

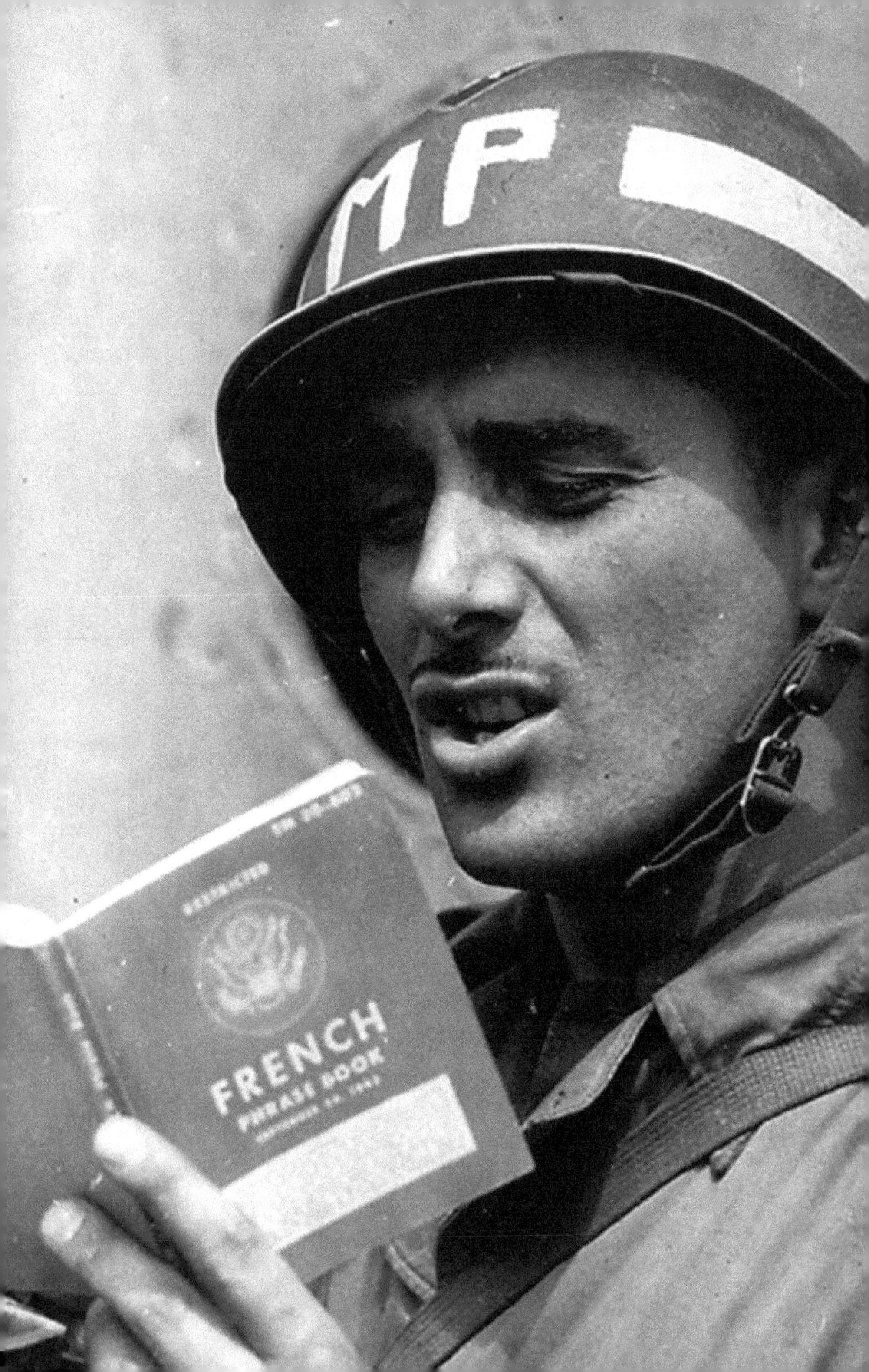
MP
FRENCH
PHRASE BOOK

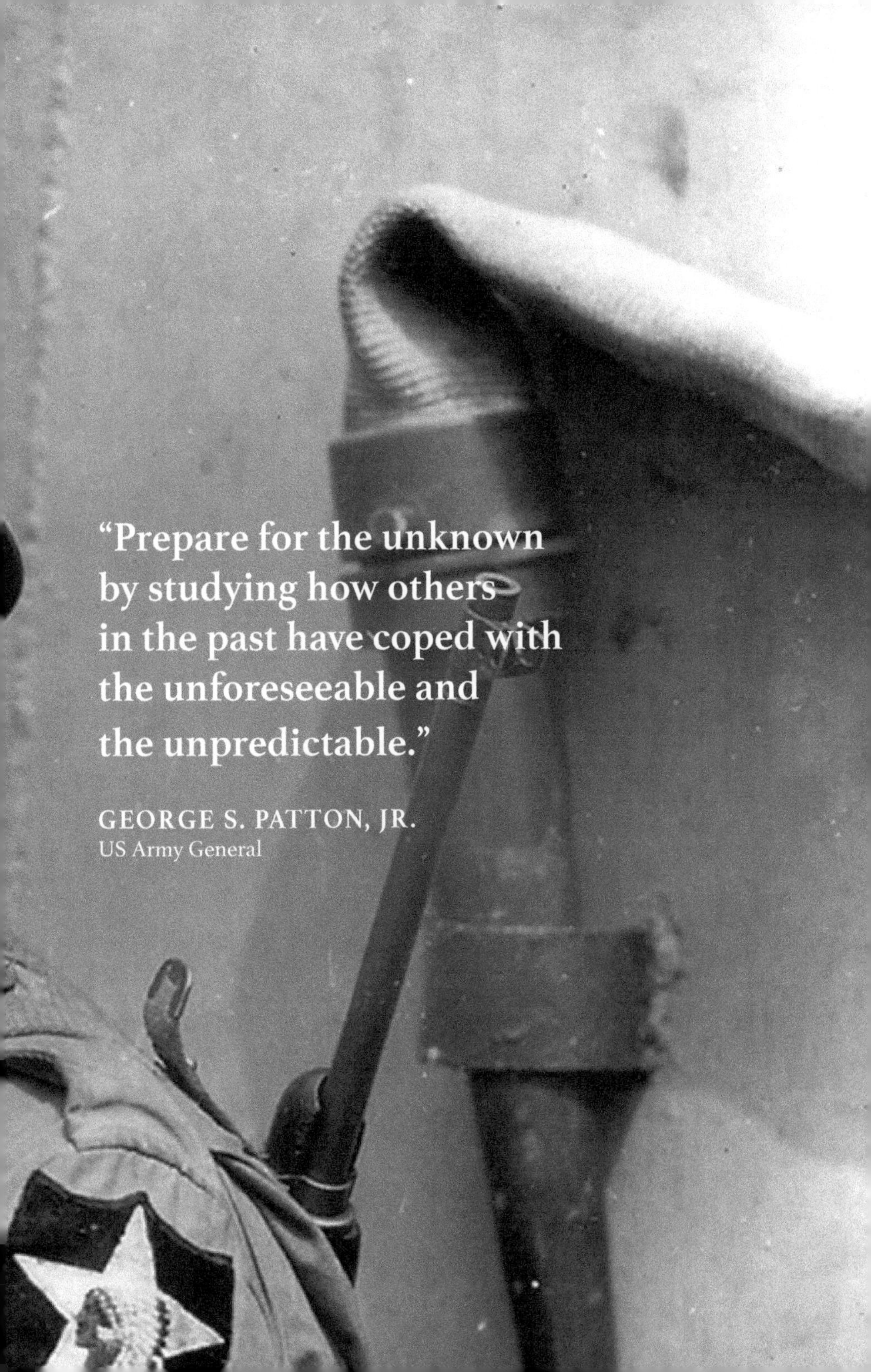

"Prepare for the unknown by studying how others in the past have coped with the unforeseeable and the unpredictable."

GEORGE S. PATTON, JR.
US Army General

What can we learn
from D-Day?

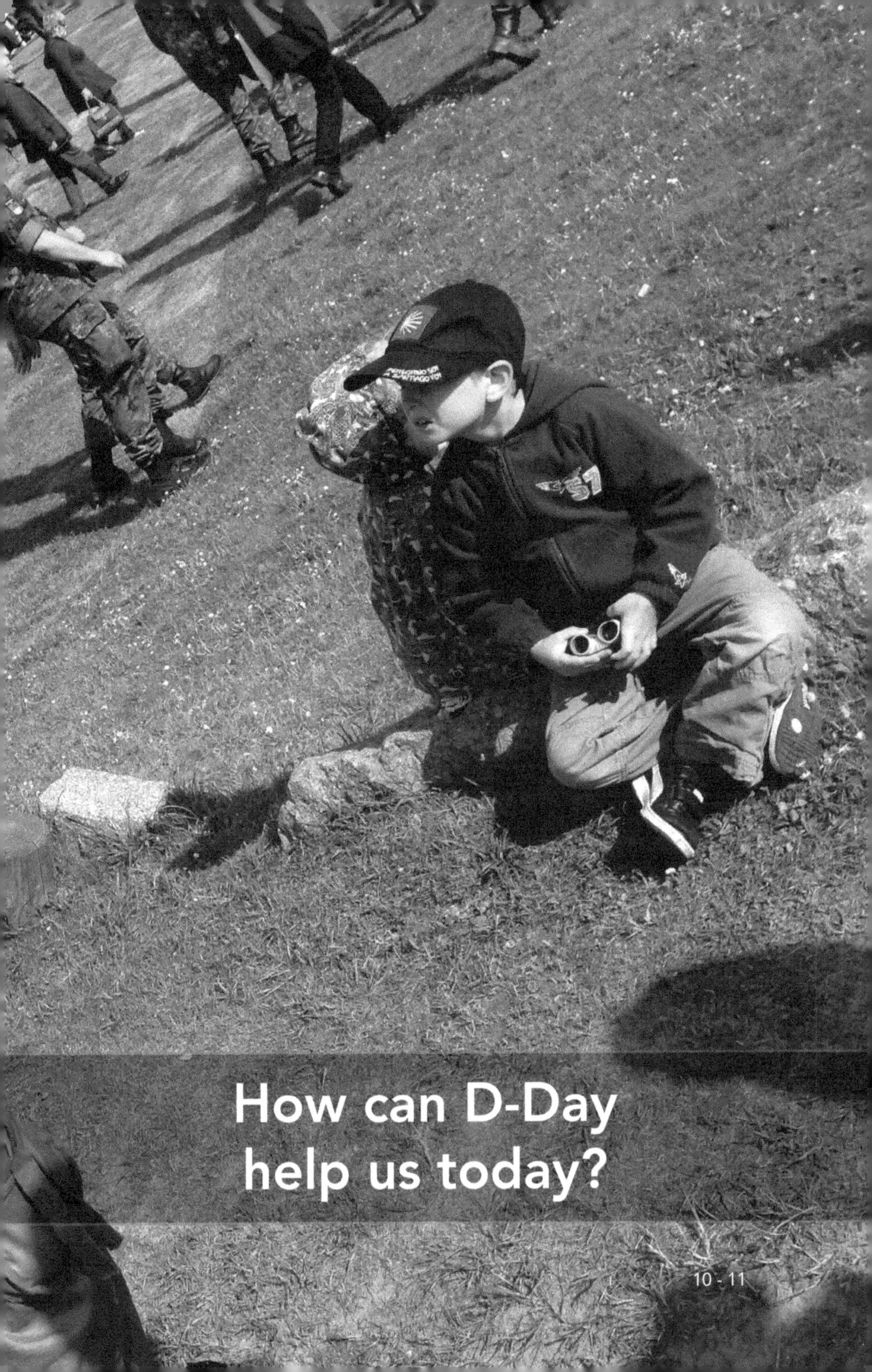

How can D-Day help us today?

D-DAY LESSONS FOR TODAY

How to Create Your Future History

Erin Meyer Charneux

First printing, 2018
ISBN 9-7890826946-0-4
Published by The School of Intuition sprl
www.erinmeyercharneux.com

To you

and our future history

Attention!

You are about to travel through time.
On your journey, you will hear multiple stories and voices, weaving through the past, present, and future.

You will encounter thought-provoking texts, juxtaposed with images to create new perspectives and insights with each viewing.

Read this book front to back...or not.
Read it once, or a million times.
Pass it on, or treasure it forever.

This book is
a compass to guide you on your journey,
a light in dark times,
a testament in itself to the efficacy of the lessons.

Let the journey begin...

As a young history student, I loved to listen to WWII veterans. In my early 20s, I was the age they had been during the war. The past was no longer a list of dates in a dusty textbook. It walked alongside me.

HISTORY became HIS STORY...

...HERS...THEIRS...OURS...

Their stories shaped their lives.

They would shape mine.

JUNE 1994
50th Anniversary of D-Day
Omaha Beach, Normandy, France

"How did the veterans' stories change your life, Erin?" Katie Couric asked me live on the American national TV program The Today Show.

"I changed my major to encompass the Second World War. I want to obtain my PhD in history and focus on how history is taught."

Life, of course, had other plans...

Curiosity lured me out of my native Texas. Love settled me in Belgium. Over 20 years later, I found myself with four bi-lingual and multicultural children. On one of our regular beach vacations in Normandy, my oldest daughter climbed down off a tank and asked, “What happened here?”

What do I want my kids to learn about the past?

How can the past help them today?

Every story lives within a larger story.
To understand the relevance of D-Day today,
one must travel back in time.

What led to D-Day?

Germany suffered from political and economic instability after WWI. Extreme right political parties used this situation to gain support from hungry and unhappy people. Adolf Hitler, leader of the National Socialist, or Nazi, Party, became Chancellor in 1933. He attracted many followers with his powerful speeches and propaganda. Hitler believed in the superiority of the Aryan race and blamed Jews and communists for Germany's problems.

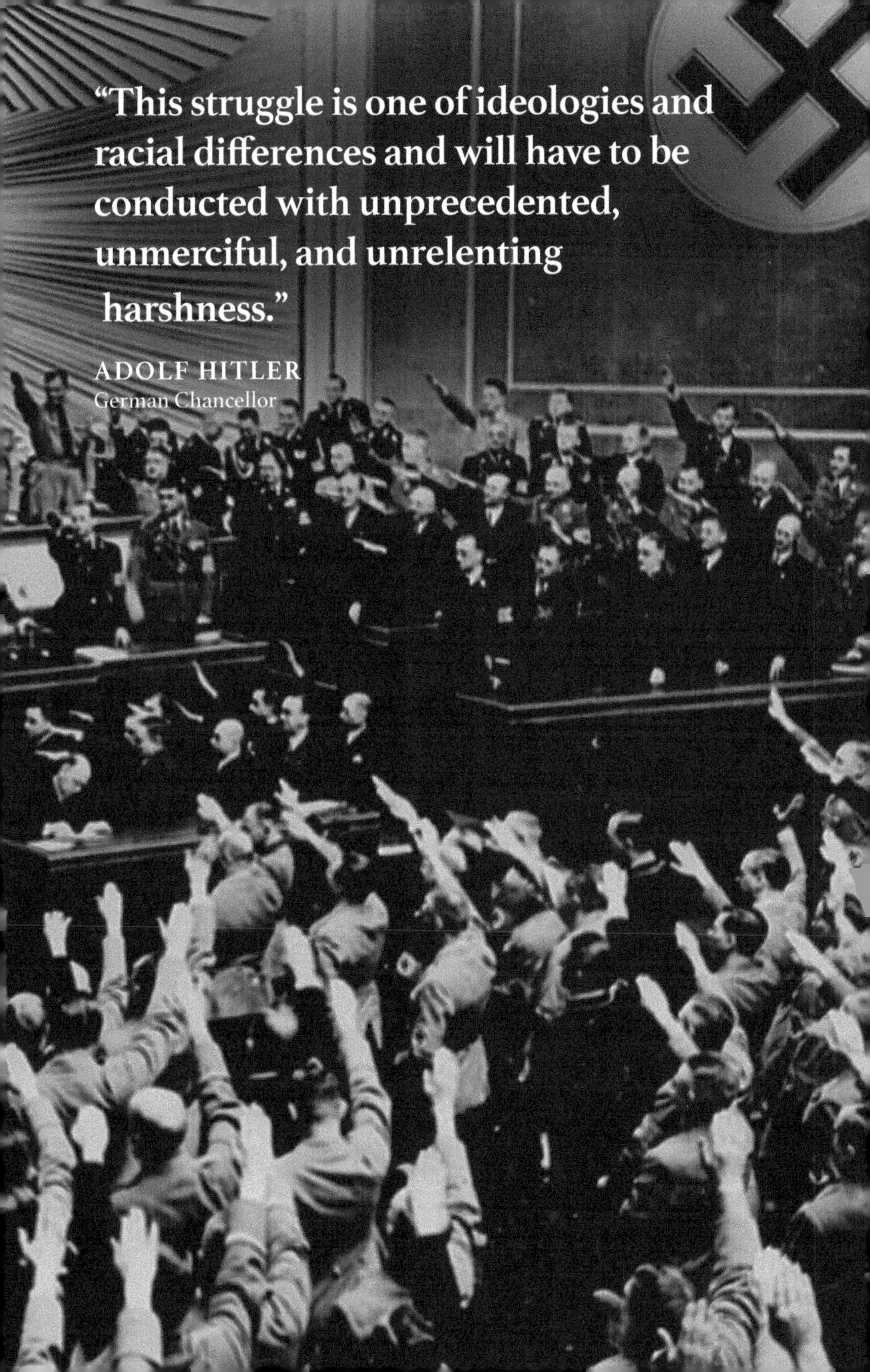

"This struggle is one of ideologies and racial differences and will have to be conducted with unprecedented, unmerciful, and unrelenting harshness."

ADOLF HITLER
German Chancellor

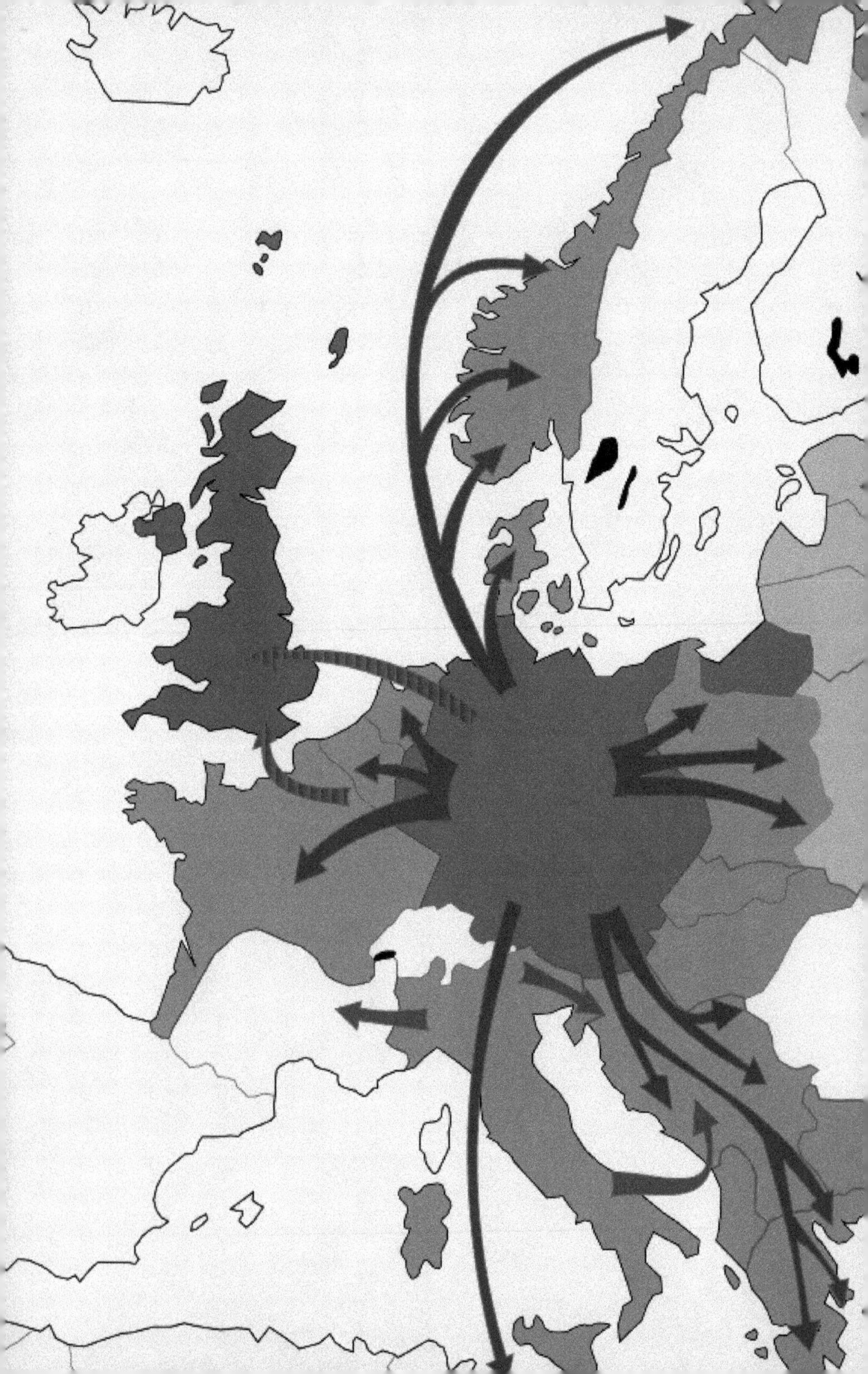

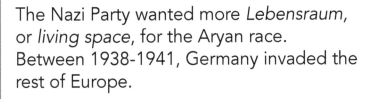

The Nazi Party wanted more *Lebensraum*, or *living space*, for the Aryan race. Between 1938-1941, Germany invaded the rest of Europe.

Twenty-three years after the end of WWI, the "war to end all wars," the world was at war again. The Axis Powers (led by Germany, Italy, and Japan) fought against the Allied Powers (led by the United Kingdom, the United States of America, and the Soviet Union).

The Nazis applied their policies of ethnic cleansing to all local populations in the occupied territories.

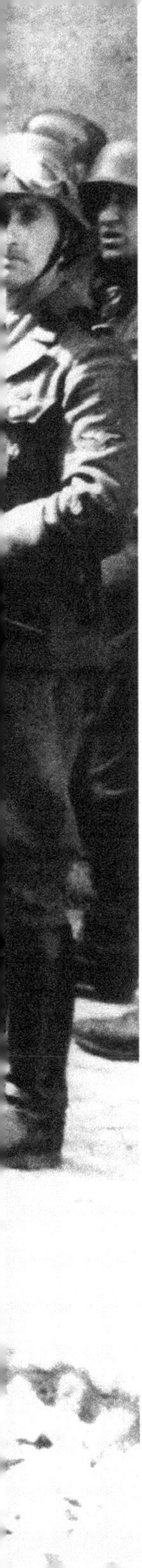

“Rats, bugs, and fleas also occur naturally; just like the Jews and Gypsies, all life is a struggle. That is why we must gradually biologically eradicate all these pests, and today that means so fundamentally changing their living conditions through preventive detention and sterilization laws that all these enemies of our people are slowly but surely eradicated.”

DR. KAREL HANNEMANN
Journal of the German Medical Association 1938

“For evil to triumph, it is only necessary for good men to do nothing.”

EDMUND BURKE
British political statesman
1729-1797

By late 1941, most of Europe was occupied by the Axis Powers.

The war on the eastern front was particularly brutal. Millions of soldiers and civilians were killed. Hitler began systematically executing people he deemed racially inferior.

Opening a second front in the West and forcing Hitler to divide his armies appeared to be the only way to defeat the German Army.

To cross the English Channel and land in France seemed the obvious way, but it posed a myriad of challenges.

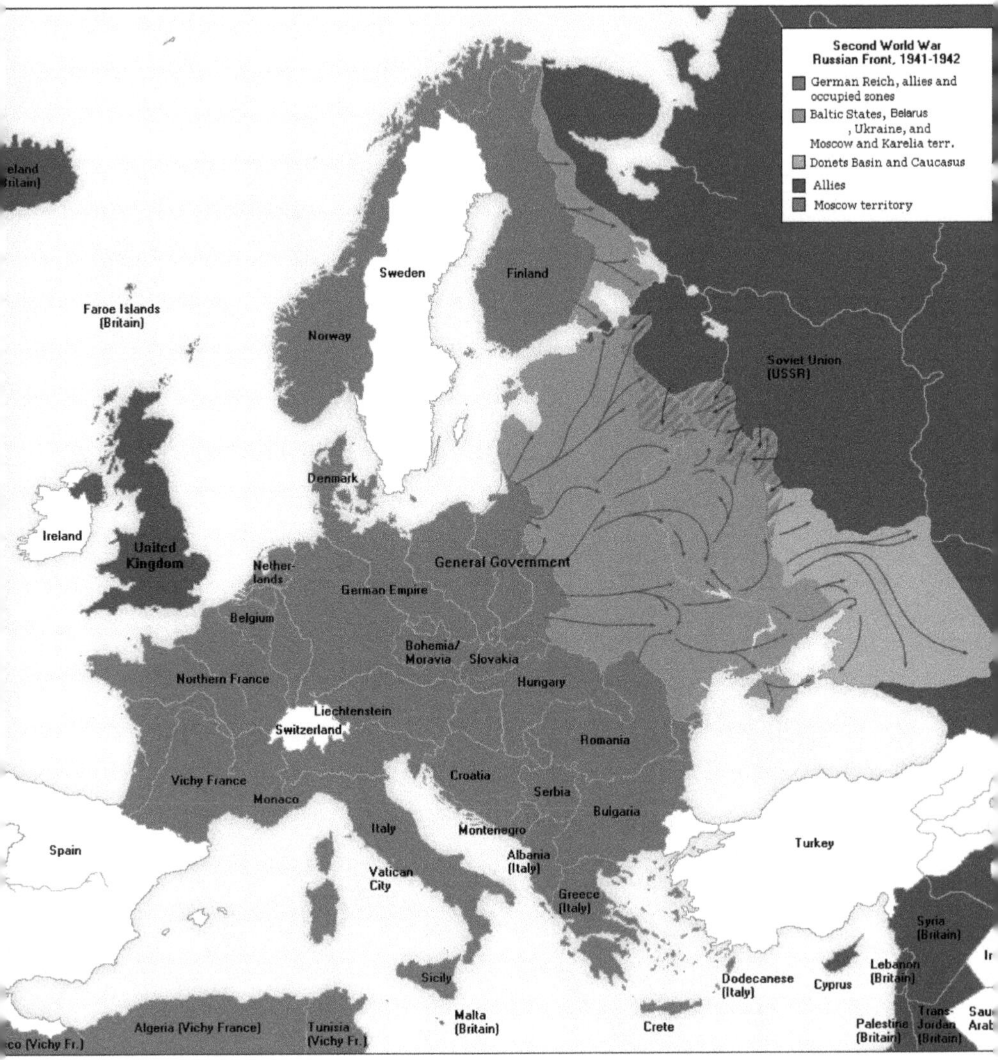
Second World War
Russian Front, 1941-1942
German Reich, allies and occupied zones
Baltic States, Belarus , Ukraine, and Moscow and Karelia terr.
Donets Basin and Caucasus
Allies
Moscow territory
Sweden
Finland
Faroe Islands (Britain)
Norway
Soviet Union (USSR)
Denmark
Ireland
United Kingdom
Nether-lands
General Government
German Empire
Belgium
Bohemia/ Moravia
Slovakia
Northern France
Hungary
Liechtenstein
Switzerland
Romania
Vichy France
Croatia
Monaco
Serbia
Bulgaria
Italy
Montenegro
Spain
Turkey
Albania (Italy)
Vatican City
Greece (Italy)
Syria (Britain)
Lebanon (Britain)
Sicily
Dodecanese (Italy)
Cyprus
Malta (Britain)
Algeria (Vichy France)
Tunisia (Vichy Fr.)
Crete
Palestine (Britain)
Trans-Jordan (Britain)

Sometimes the challenge you face is greater than anything you ever imagined.

How can you achieve something when your current circumstances deem it impossible?

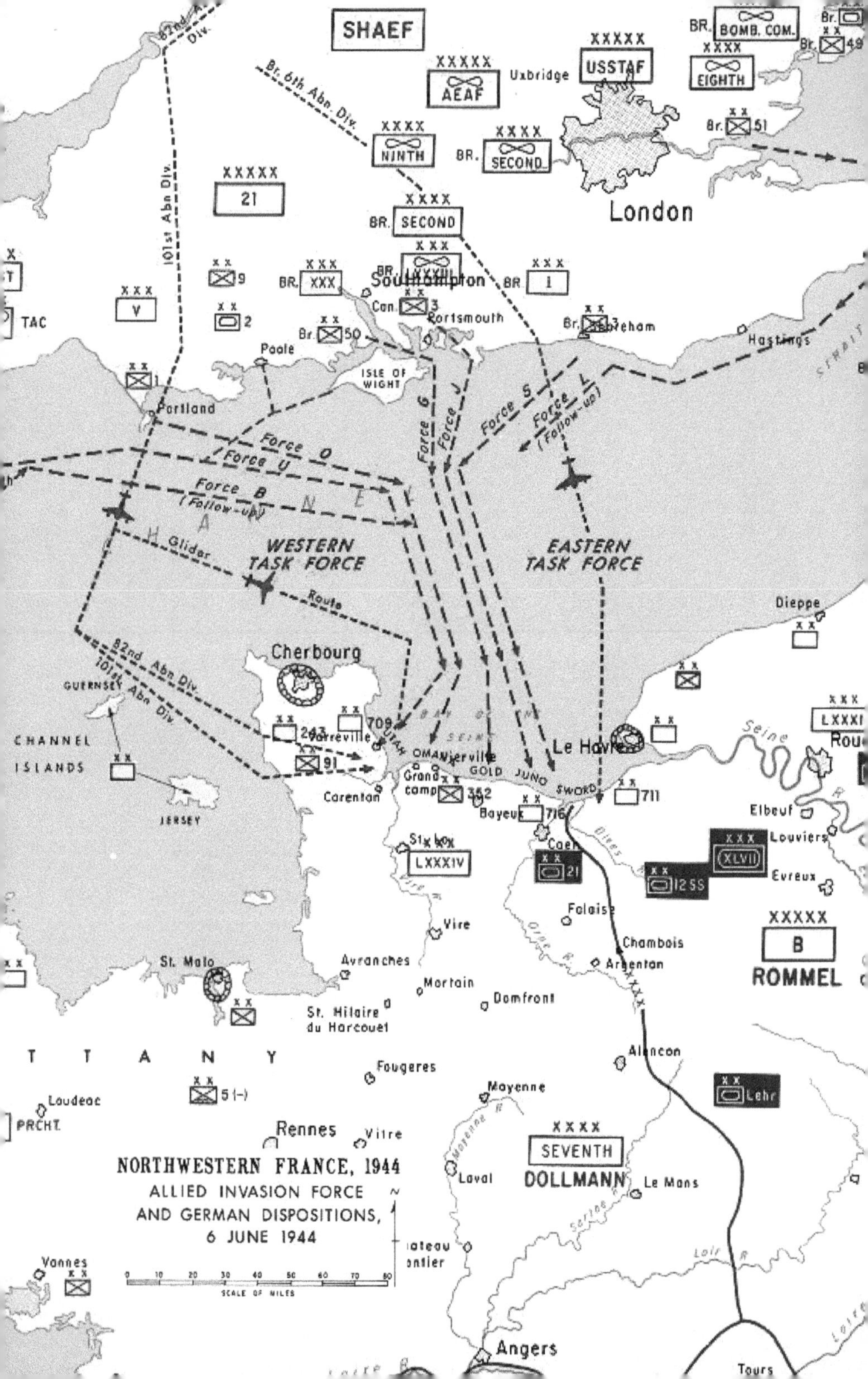

NORTHWESTERN FRANCE, 1944
ALLIED INVASION FORCE
AND GERMAN DISPOSITIONS,
6 JUNE 1944

Faced with an impossible situation, the Allies crafted their response. On the morning of June 6, 1944, forces from land and sea descended upon Normandy, France. One hundred fifty-six thousand soldiers from the Allied nations took the Germans by surprise. Within days, they established a strong footing on the European continent and began liberating Europe from German occupation.

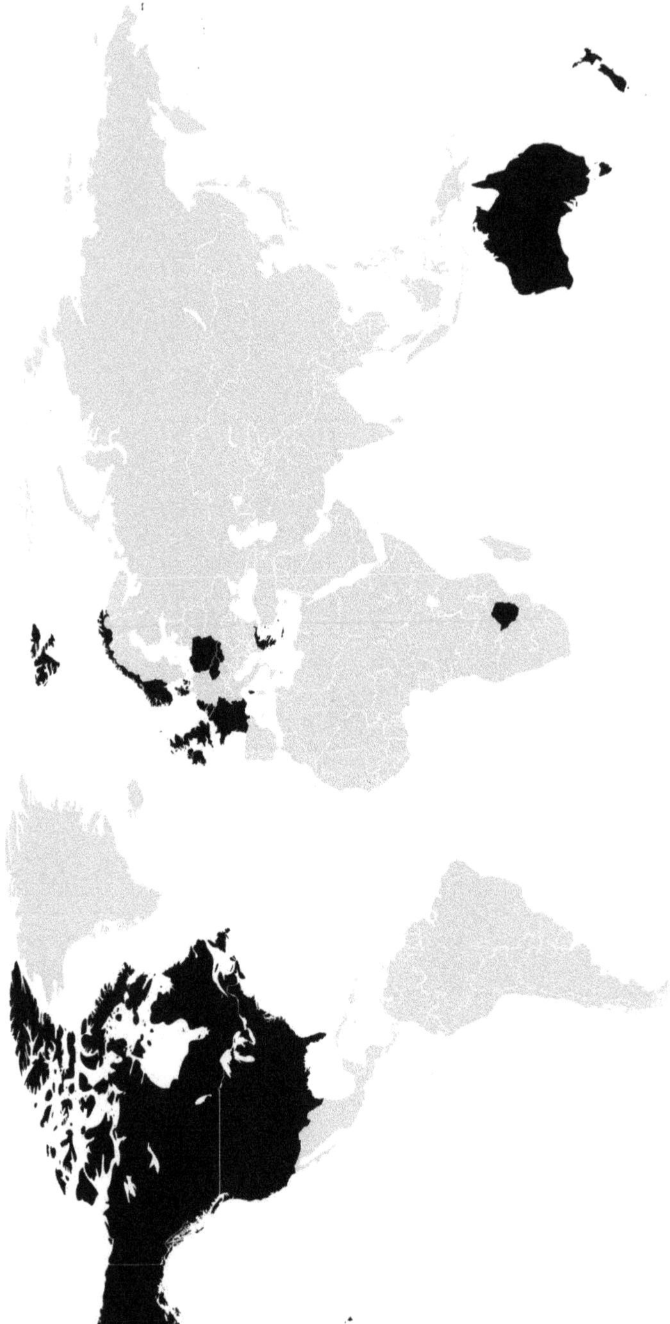

Under the direction of SHAEF (Supreme Headquarters Allied Expeditionary Force), soldiers from 14 countries participated in the D-Day landings.

Australia, Belgium, Canada, Czechoslovakia, Denmark, France, Greece, Netherlands, New Zealand, Norway, Poland, Southern Rhodesia, the United Kingdom, and the United States of America.

“Oh Kitty, the best part of the invasion is that I have a feeling that friends are on the way.”

Anne Frank
Diary entry on June 6, 1944

US
US
US

Looking back, it is hard to imagine that D-Day could have failed and the Allies could have lost the war, but nothing was certain at the time.

There were great risks involved. Significant sacrifices were made to liberate Europe from the Nazi regime.

UNITED
LESLIE RAGAN
THE UNITED NATIONS FIGHT FOR FREEDOM

No matter how each country tells its story, D-Day and the entire war was won by the joint efforts of citizens from diverse nations, fighting together.

Supreme Allied Commander of SHAEF, **GENERAL DWIGHT D. EISENHOWER,** explains this concept in a radio broadcast on June 6, 1944:

"People of Western Europe. A landing was made this morning on the coast of France by troops of the Allied Expeditionary Force. This landing is part of the concerted United Nations plan for the liberation of Europe, made in conjunction with our great Russian allies.

I have this message for all of you. Although the initial assault may not have been made in your own country, the hour of your liberation is approaching.

All patriots, men and women, young and old, have a part to play in the achievement of final victory."

It was an audacious feat, which required commitment with no guarantee of success.

Operation Overlord, more commonly known as D-Day, is an iconic event in the history of WWII.

D-Day continues to be commemorated each year by world leaders and individual citizens alike.

POLICE

The war was won through the personal leadership and innovative vision of individual citizens and soldiers, working together for a greater good.

D-Day was conceived in an unstable world, facing an unpredictable future.

Studying how people from the past chose their response and how they created their future history, we discover a compass to guide us as we create our lives today.

D-DAY LESSONS

1. History is full of people doing "the impossible."

2. Know what you stand for.

3. Creativity reaches far beyond a frame on the wall.

4. To get good answers, ask good questions.

5. To get where you want to go, locate yourself on the map.

FOR TODAY

6. Know how to recognize your allies.

7. To win the war, learn from battles lost.

8. Go to the edge of the hedge.

9. Honor their lives by living yours.

10. Freedom is not controlling the content of your life. Freedom is creating the context.

1

History is full of people doing "the impossible."

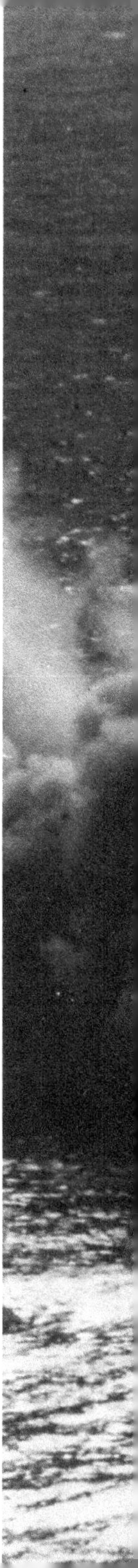

In January 1943, United States President Franklin Roosevelt and United Kingdom Prime Minister Sir Winston Churchill met at the Casablanca Conference to determine a common Anglo-American strategy for the war.

They officially decided to land on the beaches of France. This would open a second front in the west and bring the fight to Germany.

At the time, however, it seemed far from possible.

German U-boats dominated the Atlantic. The Allies lacked the air supremacy necessary for a beach landing. The technology to land and supply an army did not yet exist.

In 1066, William the Conqueror made one of the most famous crossings of the English Channel.

64 - 65

The Allies would be attempting a sea landing on a scale never before seen in history.

PA13-22
US 489
US

PISTOL PAC
MAMA

"Risk more
than others think is safe.

Care more
than others think is wise.

Dream more
than others think is practical.

Expect more
than others think is possible."

Cadets' maxim at
US Military Academy West Point

In January 1943, Churchill and Roosevelt declared that they would make the impossible possible despite the fact that they did not yet have the necessary technology, manpower nor strategic position.

There is power in telling your intentions to the world.

Write them down.

Commit to them.

“You must
do the things
you think
you cannot do.”

ELEANOR ROOSEVELT

US First Lady

A professor once told me that I should write a book instead of getting a PhD. I liked the idea so much that I put it way up high on a shelf where no one could reach it, not even me. I stopped my PhD to have my first child and never looked back. Then one day, while rummaging through my shelves, my book idea fell down and hit me on the head. Who, me? So much has been written about D-Day. What could I add to the dialogue? Could I approach it from a completely different angle?

Thinking I was probably jumping into waters way over my head, I decided to at least go exploring in Normandy. My son told his teacher why I was gone. "I didn't know you were a writer," she exclaimed upon my return. "Neither did I!" I wanted to respond. My son's declaration had made my idea public. What I had once believed impossible was beginning to shift.

IMPOSSIBLE can become I'M POSSIBLE

A change in perspective changes everything.

What is your current version of "impossible"

?

2

Know what you stand for.

MUNE D'AIREL
SEANCES
RECREATIVES

Pursuing "the impossible" requires commitment and perseverance. You must know why you are doing it.

Declaring what you stand for enables others to stand with you.

LONG LIVE AMERICA
THE FRENCH ARE THANKFUL

LONG LIVE LIBERTY
TO THE AMERICAN SOLDIERS
C. PUZENAT
EN VENTE ICI

In the spring of 1944, weeks away from launching the Normandy landings, Supreme Commander of the Allied Expeditionary Force, Dwight D. "Ike" Eisenhower, made an impromptu speech to the graduating class of the British Royal Military Academy at Sandhurst. Considered one of his best speeches, Ike made it clear that each individual's happiness and freedom depended on the success of D-Day.

THIS SYNAGOGUE
WILL BE OPEN FOR 24 HOURS
FOR
SPECIAL SERVICES ON "D" DAY

"You are about to embark upon the Great Crusade toward which we have striven these many months. The eyes of the world are upon you. The hopes and prayers of liberty-loving people everywhere march with you."

DWIGHT D. EISENHOWER
Supreme Commander's letter to soldiers, June 6, 1944

192255

"They fight not for
the lust of conquest.
They find to end conquest.
They fight to liberate."

FRANKLIN D. ROOSEVELT
US President radio broadcast, June 6, 1944

Venturing into the unknown is scary. Knowing why you do something can help you move forward alongside your fear and even help you to make light of it.

“If you’re going through hell,
keep going.”
SIR WINSTON CHURCHILL
UK Prime Minister

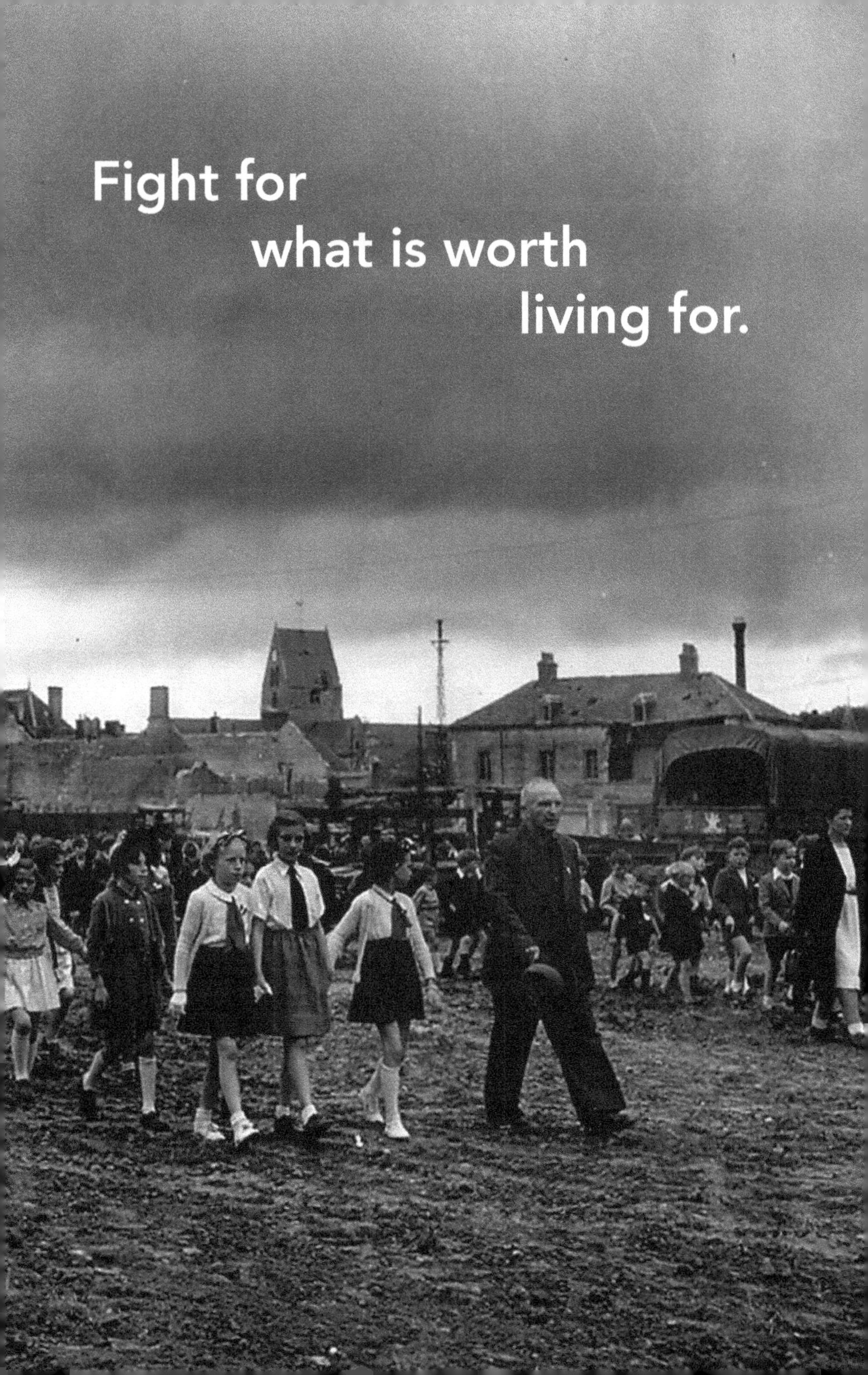
Fight for
what is worth
living for.

I never expected to develop such a deep fascination for WWII history. I do not come from a military family nor did any of my close relatives fight in the war. Following my curiosity, however, has taken me down many unexpected and amazing paths. The boots I stepped into in order to write this book felt way too big when I started, but I wanted to answer my daughter's question about Normandy. I wanted to tell her why it was important, both for her and for myself.

Every "impossible" journey needs a why. The Why grabs the steering wheel and pushes Fear to the back seat.

I wrote this book for my children. It is the story of my own journey, a compass to guide them on their own expeditions through life.

A vision greater than yourself. A world of possibilities and doubts.
A voice shouts through the darkness, "What makes you think you can do that?"
Whether or not you can is beside the point.

If you don't know why, you may never try.

What do you stand for

?

3

Creativity
reaches
far beyond
a frame
on the wall.

These generals knew there were many obstacles to overcome for a successful beach landing.

Q: How do you provide fuel for an invading army?

A: P.L.U.T.O.
(Pipe Line Under The Ocean)

Q: How do you fake an invasion in one area while the real one happens elsewhere?

A: Create a Ghost Army led by a famous general equipped with inflatable tanks and artificial sounds.

77

Q: How can you make it seem like you have more soldiers than you actually do?

A: Drop "Ruperts" over Normandy and the Pas-de-Calais equipped with boots, helmets, and speakers projecting combat noises, mortar explosions, and sounds of soldiers cursing.

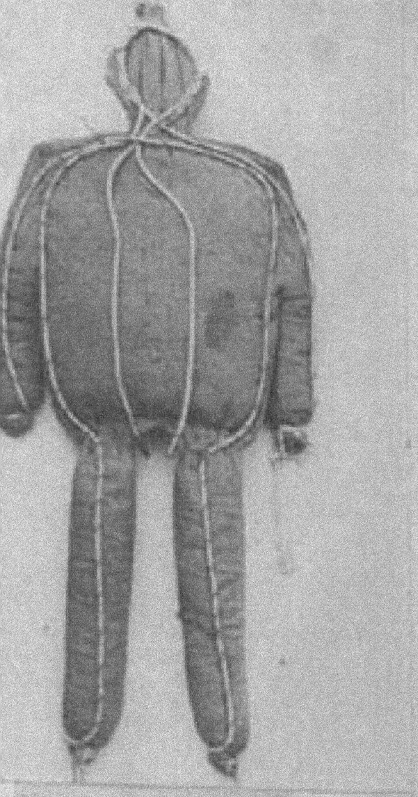

Self destroying version(SDV)

SDV with rifle fire simulation

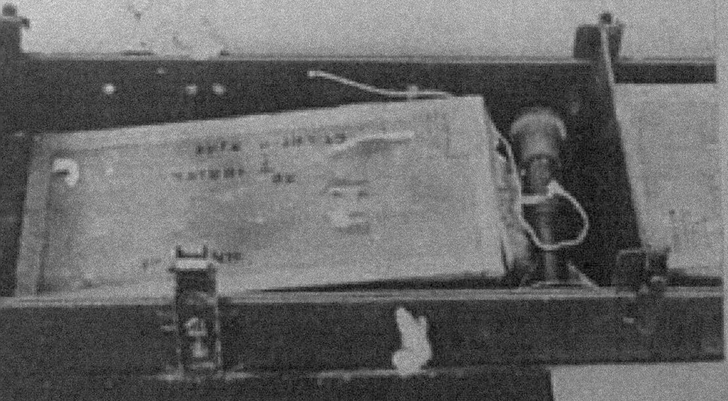

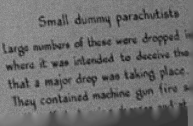

Small dummy parachutists

Large numbers of these were dropped i

where it was intended to deceive the

that a major drop was taking place.

They contained machine gun fire s

Creative problem-solving
doesn’t mean
reinventing the wheel.
Look for new ways to use
existing resources.
Dare to do the unexpected.

Thinking like everyone else
isn't necessarily *thinking*.

"I'm not creative," I used to say. "That title is worn by my sister, the successful fashion designer." "What? That's crazy, Erin. Of course you're creative!" my sister replied one day. "What about the way you designed your own degree in college? The way you created a life in another country? The way you can make dinner out of 'nothing' in the fridge?"

"Oh...I never thought of it that way..."

Creativity is more than making a piece of art to hang on a wall. It is how we approach life; how we face daily challenges; the choices we make or do not make. Creativity thrives on a change in perspective and the freeing of our mind. Consciously or not, we create each day of our lives.

Shifting sands and swift tides are a fact of life.

Creativity is the key to navigating the world today.

How can you use existing resources in new, unexpected ways

?

4

To get good answers, ask good questions.

Many walls have been built throughout history out of fear, anger, or insecurity. They rarely withstand the test of time. Hitler tried to defend the entire coastline of Europe from Norway to Spain with his Atlantic Wall. The Allies knew from experience that attacking this wall at its most heavily defended points would not be successful.

How can a wall be made obsolete?

The Allies' first challenge was to land an army on the beaches of Normandy. Nearly as important, they needed to supply soldiers and reinforce their numbers as they continued to move inland.

The Allies needed a port.

The failed raid on the port of Dieppe in August 1942 proved that attacking Hitler's Atlantic Wall head-on would not work.
What if the Allies brought a port with them?

There were many who believed it could not be done, but Churchill framed the challenge perfectly in the following memo:

10, Downing Street,
Whitehall.

PIERS FOR USE ON BEACHES

C.C.O.
or deputy.

They must float up and down with the tide. The anchor problem must be mastered. Let me have the best solution worked out. Don't argue the matter. The difficulties will argue for themselves.

30. 5. 42.

Churchill did not ask
IF it were possible.

He asked
HOW.

Operational just three days after D-Day, Port Winston was created off the beach of Arromanches-les-Bains. The floating harbor was an incredible engineering feat. Old battleships were sunk to create breakwaters. Enormous cement caissons, several stories high, were built in England and towed across the Channel. The innovative technology used to create the floating platforms is still used today in oil rigs at sea.

Churchill's question enabled an "impossible" innovation. The German defenses were made irrelevant through "A single, brilliant technical device,"declared Albert Speer, German Minister for Armament and War Production.

Wreckage of aging caissons sits off the beach of Arromanches as a testament to the power of creative thinking.

No matter how high or wide a wall, there is always a way to move past it. Built to withstand brute force, walls are made obsolete by open minds asking the right questions.

"We cannot solve our problems with the same kind of thinking we used when we created them."

ALBERT EINSTEIN
German-born theoretical physicist

507
A-BT

I knew what. I knew why. I didn't know how.
It would not be easy to find time for research while breastfeeding and being a full-time mom to four kids from 1 to 12 years old. I spent more time running after my children in museums than appreciating the details of a well-planned exhibit.

When I whispered, "What if…?" to my mom, she replied, "Why not?" Suddenly, I had found an ally of my own who was willing to join me on a four-hour jeep ride in the rain in the name of research.

My mother, who hiked 800km to celebrate her 70th birthday, taught me how exciting it is to ask the unexpected of myself: How can I make my own walls obsolete?

I strive to do the same for my children. I experiment on the edge of my comfort zone. I share my dreams and doubts. I let them see me afraid. Most of all, I am constantly reframing my questions.

The answers exist.
The key is knowing how to unlock them.

What
happens
when you
replace
"Can I"
with
"How can I"

?

5

To get where you want to go, locate yourself on the map.

Bad weather and strong currents pushed the first wave of landing crafts off course. Landing on Utah Beach, the Allies quickly realized they were not where they had planned to be. What to do? Put everyone back in boats, and go up the coast to land in the right location?

THEODORE ROOSEVELT, JR. was a 56 year old US Army Brigadier General who petitioned his way into the first wave of troops to land on Utah Beach. Bad eyesight, a heart condition, and a cane would not stop him.

He was among the first leaders to realize these were the wrong dunes, the wrong landmarks, and hence the wrong location.
Legend has it that he proclaimed:

"We'll just start the war from right here!"

The heart condition proved fatal when he died of a heart attack just over a month later. He was posthumously awarded the US Congressional Medal of Honor for his courageous leadership on Utah Beach.

St. Malo
Platzkommandantur
Standortkommandantur
Feldgendarmerie
Ulla
OT
FRONTLEITSTELLE
AM BAHNHOF
N.S.K.K. 64
BUNKER
Soldat
H.K.
Wehr
Nachsc

You may not be where you want to be, but where you are is the only place you can begin.

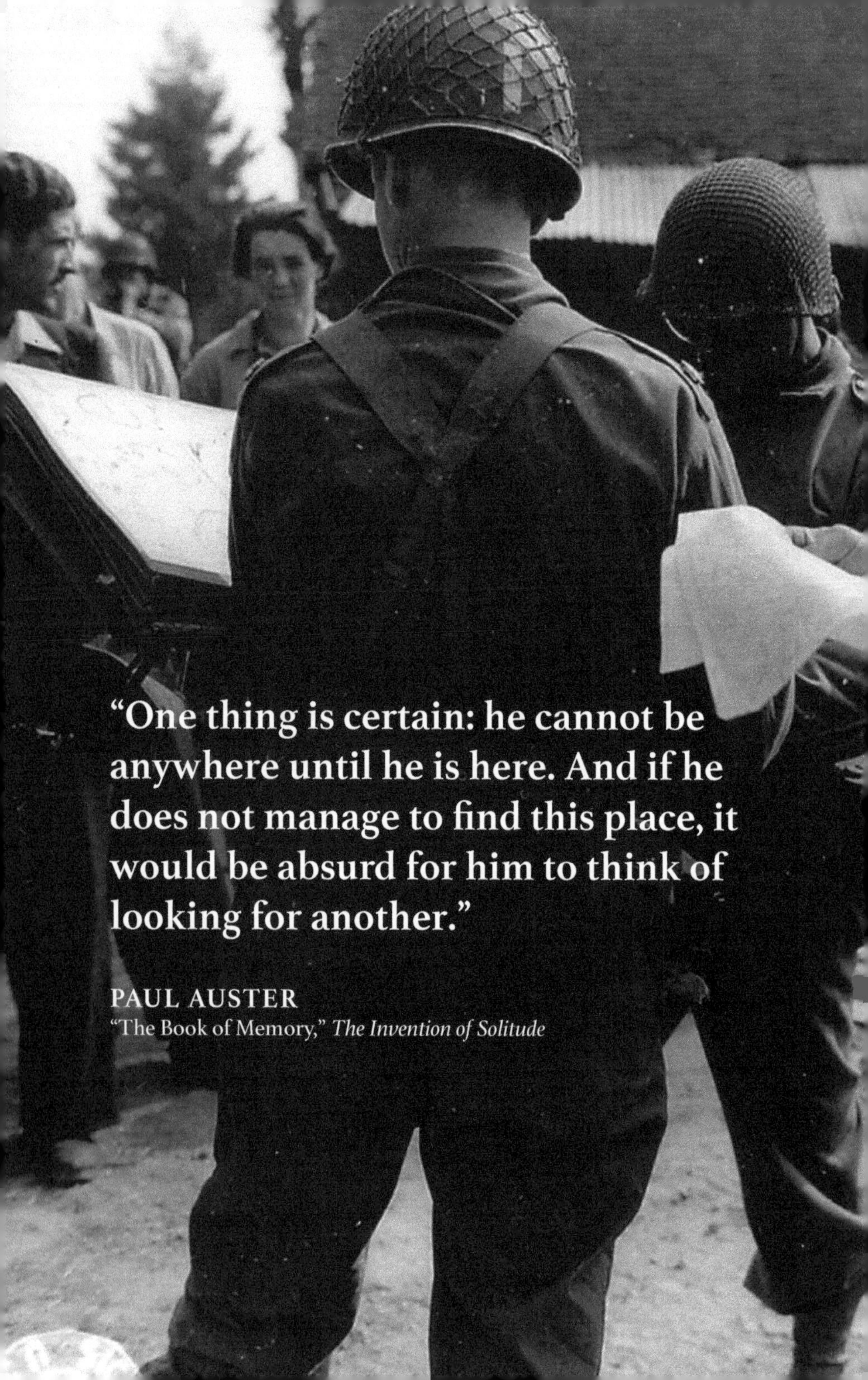

"One thing is certain: he cannot be anywhere until he is here. And if he does not manage to find this place, it would be absurd for him to think of looking for another."

PAUL AUSTER
"The Book of Memory," *The Invention of Solitude*

**Face the facts.
They face you.**

KM 00
VOIE
LIBERTE
1944
0913
UTAH BEACH
ICI
ONT DEBARQUE
LES
ARMEES AMERICAINES
6 JUIN 1944

The beginning of a book idea. A research trip.
A souvenir photo, ruined by my toddler in the foreground?
Perfect in its imperfection.

I am a mother of four, writing a book. If I deny either one of those facts, I will never get where I want to go.

The Liberty Way marks the route liberated by the US 3rd Army from June to September 1944. One marker for each of the 1,145 kilometers on the route. It begins with KM00 on Utah Beach and goes all the way to Bastogne, Belgium.

A miniature marker of KM 00 sits on my desk as a daily reminder.

Start where you are with what you have.

Where are you today

?

6

Know how to recognize your allies.

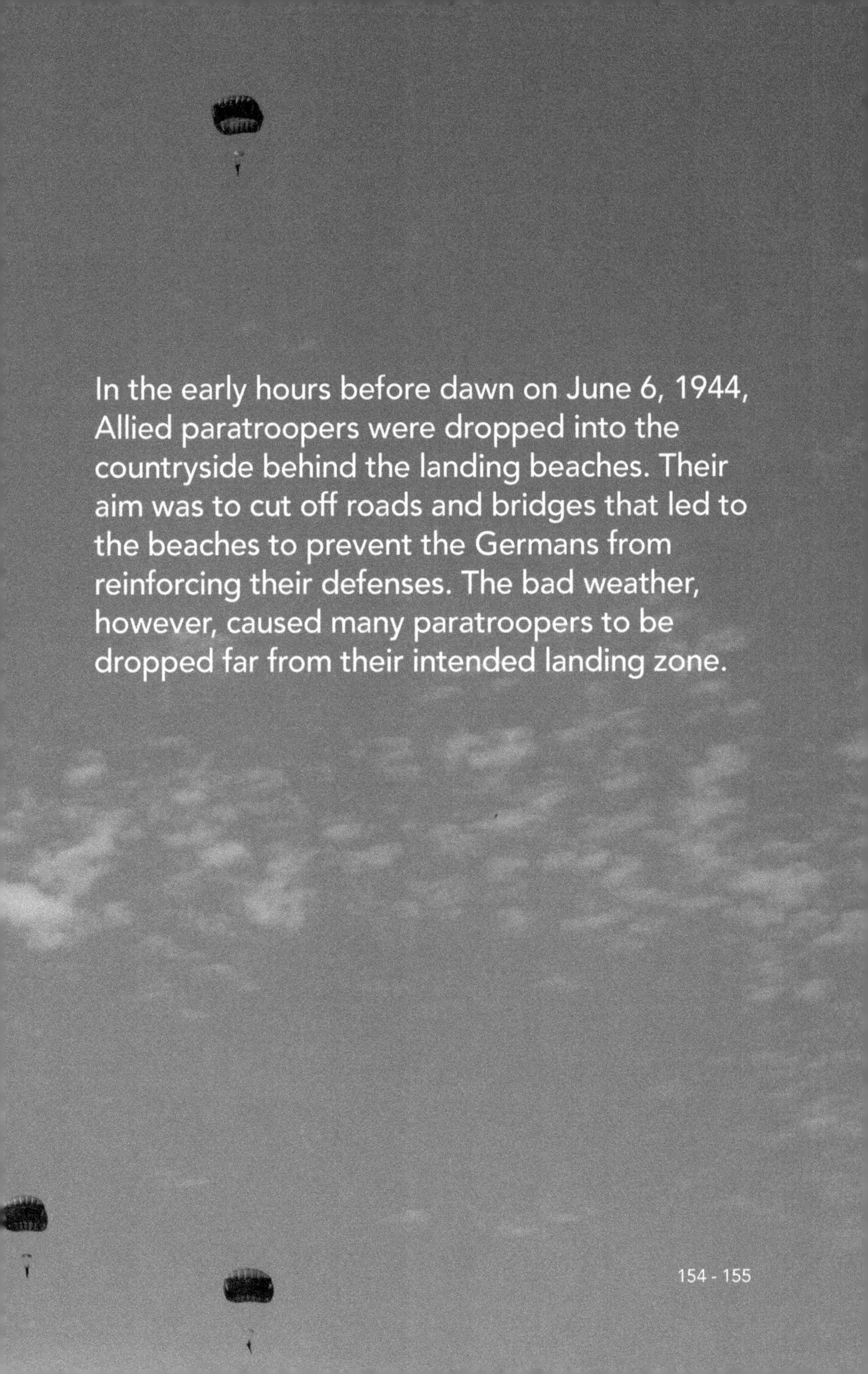

In the early hours before dawn on June 6, 1944, Allied paratroopers were dropped into the countryside behind the landing beaches. Their aim was to cut off roads and bridges that led to the beaches to prevent the Germans from reinforcing their defenses. The bad weather, however, caused many paratroopers to be dropped far from their intended landing zone.

"I wondered where the heck I was when I hit the ground. I spent all night trying to find my way in the dark toward my rendezvous point near the coast, dodging enemy patrols the whole way."

JAN DE VRIES
1st Canadian Parachute Battalion

DEBARQUEMENT

In the dark of night.
Behind enemy lines.
A movement in the bushes.

A simple handheld clicker
to know if it is a
friend or foe.

One click: Are you an ally?
Two clicks: Yes!

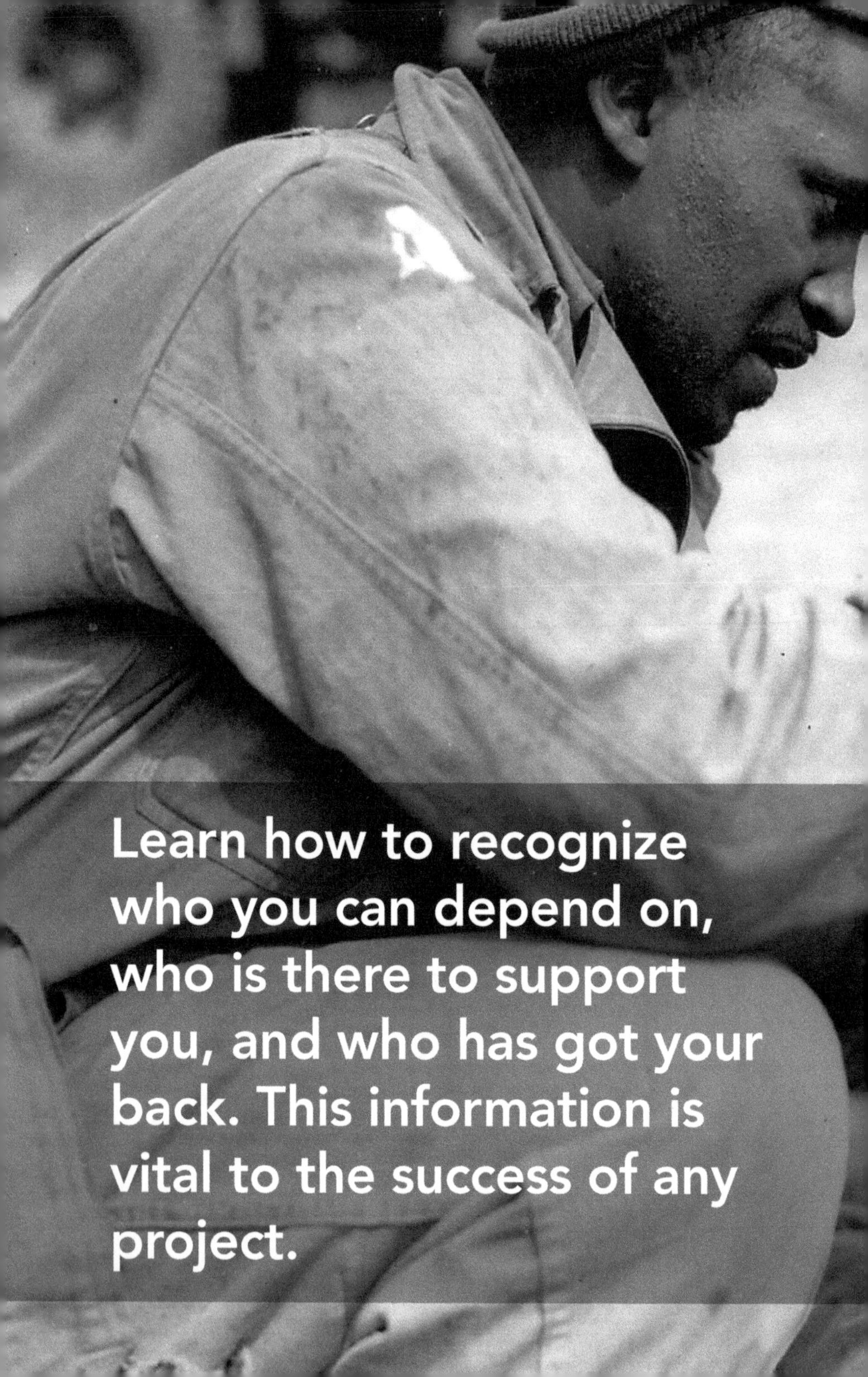
Learn how to recognize who you can depend on, who is there to support you, and who has got your back. This information is vital to the success of any project.

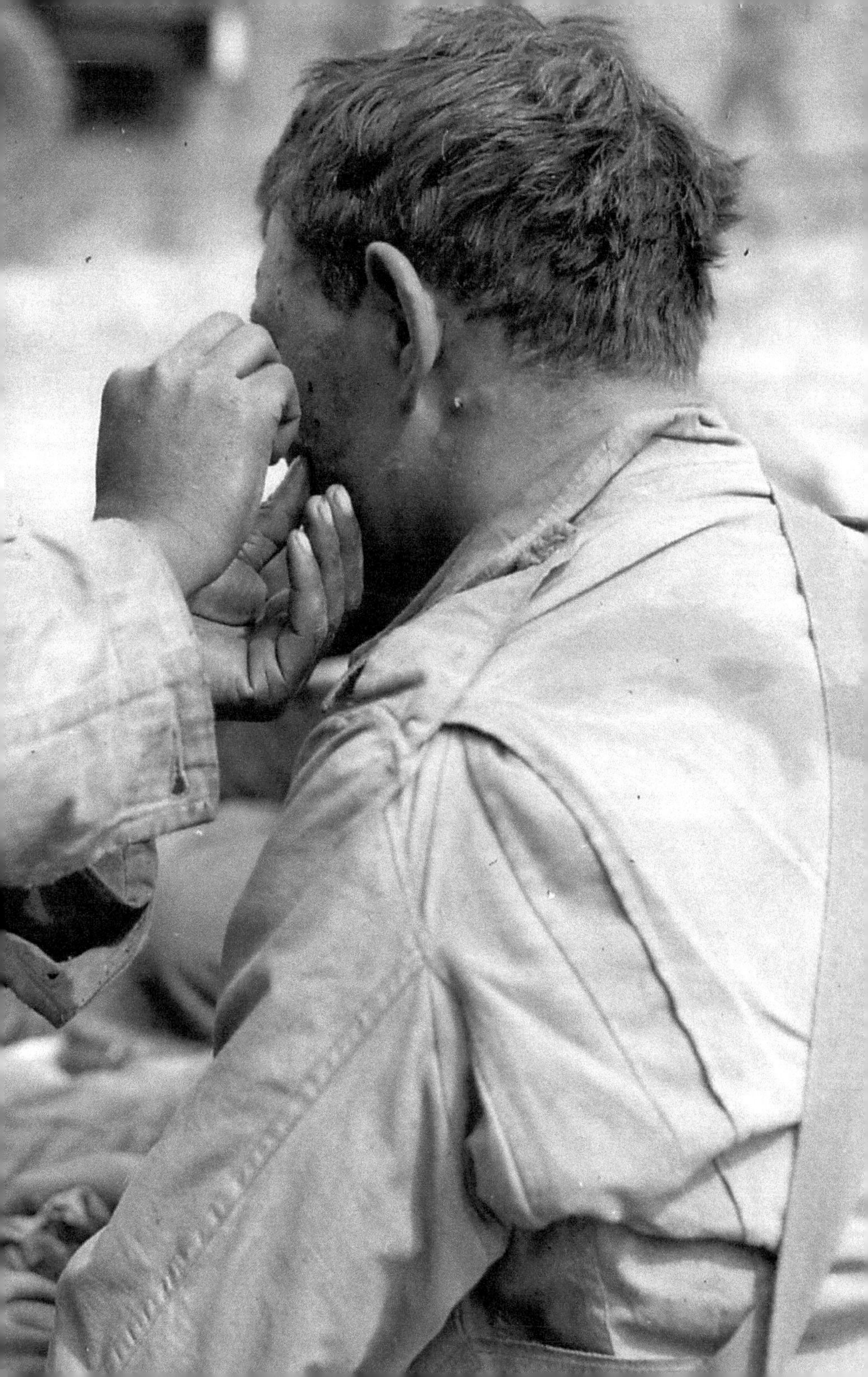

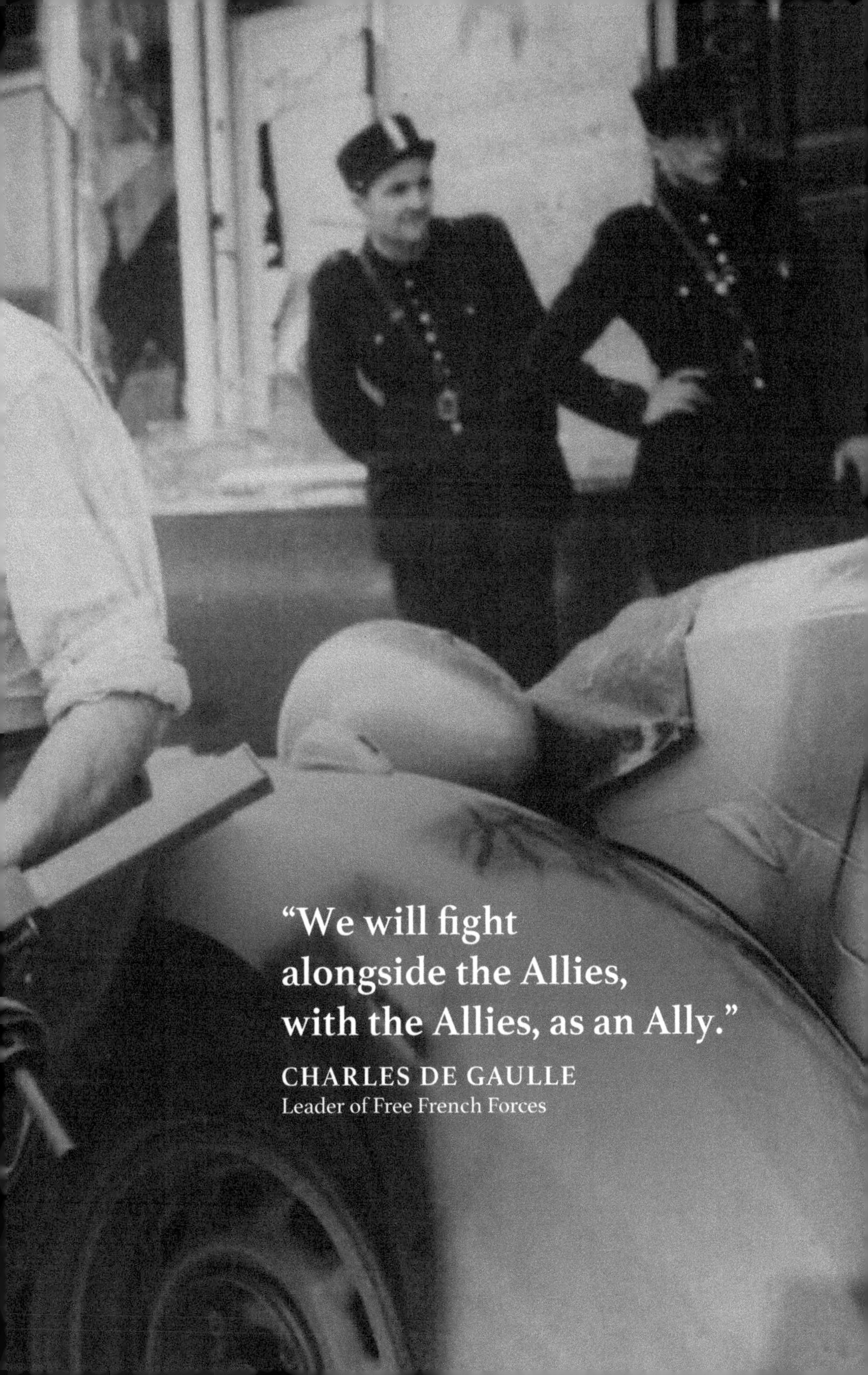

“We will fight alongside the Allies, with the Allies, as an Ally.”

CHARLES DE GAULLE
Leader of Free French Forces

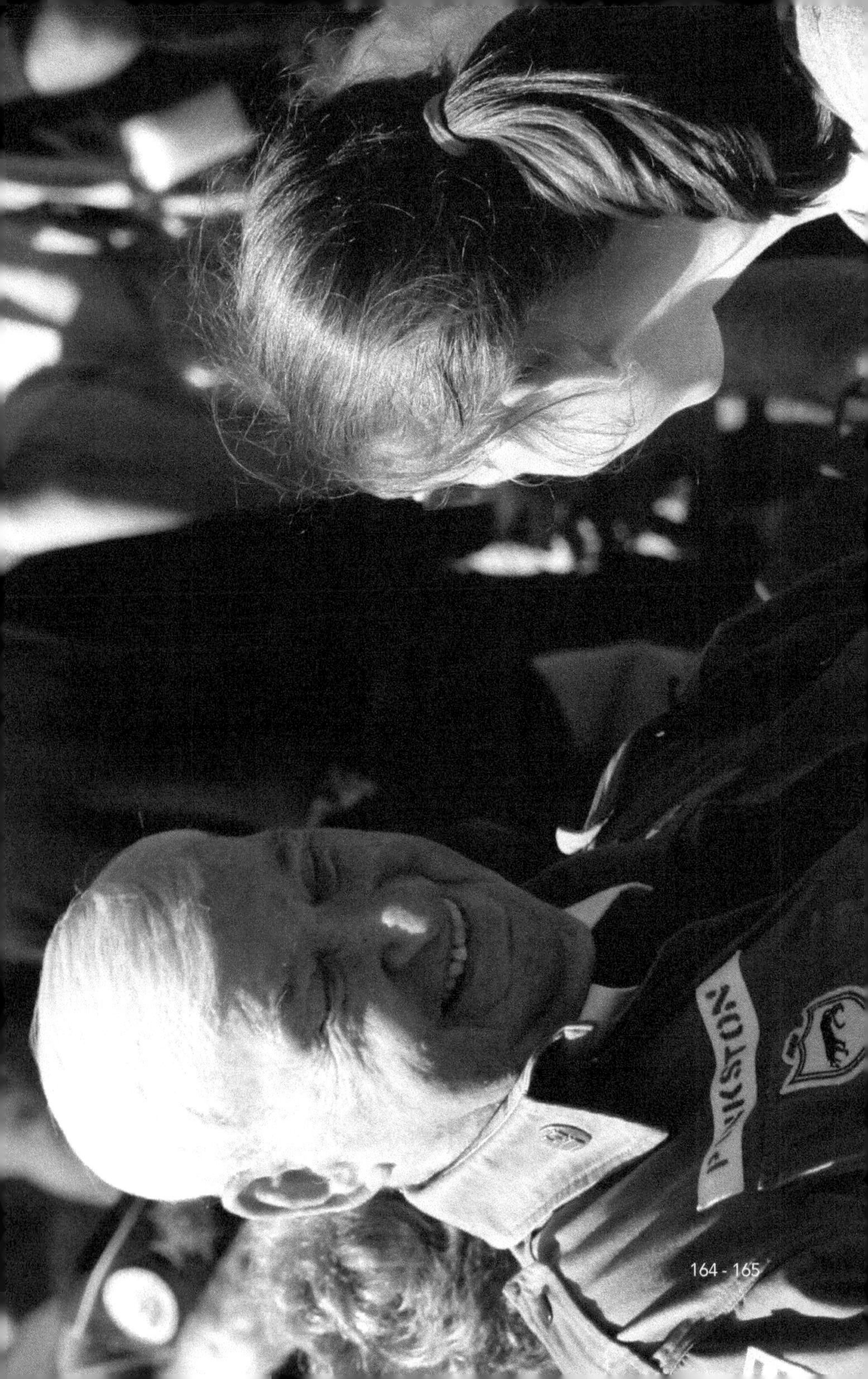

Your allies are your friends and mentors. They make all the difference when you are pursuing "the impossible." They have been there before and can offer advice. They believe you can succeed. They remind you when you forget.

Those who are not your allies have nothing to add. Worse yet, they try to make you believe you have nothing to contribute.

Allies understand when you decline an invitation because you are working in your creative cave. Allies cheer when you come out.

As a mother, I help my children recognize who truly supports them and who does not.

Anyone or anything that drains your time and energy is not your ally.

Who are your allies

?

7

To win the war, learn from battles lost.

Just as history shows us
people doing "the impossible,"
it also shows us people making mistakes.
What can we learn from our mistakes?

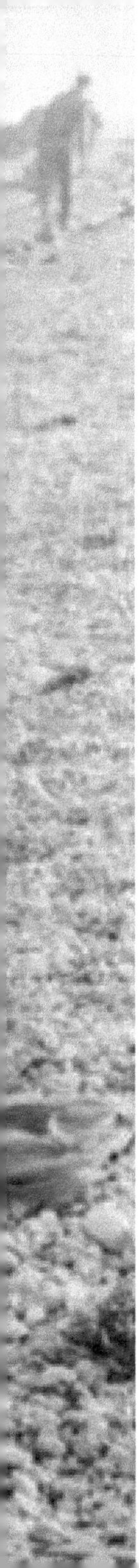

Beach landings cost lives:
Dieppe. Tarawa. Anzio.

Churchill would not forget the failed beach landing in Gallipoli during WWI.

More than 700 US soldiers died in a training exercise at Slapton Sands, England, only six weeks before D-Day.

Losses and mistakes.
Lessons written in blood.

The failed Dieppe raid inspired the floating Mulberry Harbors for D-Day. Originally, there were two harbors built on both Gold and Omaha Beaches, but a violent storm damaged both ports over June 19-22, 1944. Refusing to be defeated by uncontrollable forces, the Allies salvaged parts from the Omaha harbor to rebuild the one on Gold Beach in Arromanches.

One of the most iconic generals in history, US Army General George S. Patton, Jr. made some infamous mistakes.

After slapping a soldier in Sicily who suffered from PTSD, Patton was sidelined for D-Day. Instead, he commanded a Ghost Army "invading" near Calais. Would he be given another chance to lead?

After being hidden for several weeks in a secluded apple orchard deep in the countryside of Normandy, in July 1944, Patton launched Operation Cobra. He led the US 3rd Army across northern France to Bastogne, Belgium, and into history.

"The test of success is not what you do when you are on top. Success is how high you bounce when you hit the bottom."

GEORGE S. PATTON, JR.
US Army General

Mistakes
are the masonry
of the masterpiece.

LUCKY FORWARD

A weak first draft.
An insufficient second.
A complicated third.
An incomplete fourth....

Figure out what works by learning from what doesn't.
Multiple drafts are essential to finding your way.

Sometimes we are afraid to act for fear of falling down.
We stop, hesitate, look back, but as General Patton would say,

"There is only one direction: FORWARD!"

Do not fear making mistakes.
Failure is feedback.

What feedback can you take from your "failures"

?

8

Go to
the edge
of the
hedge.

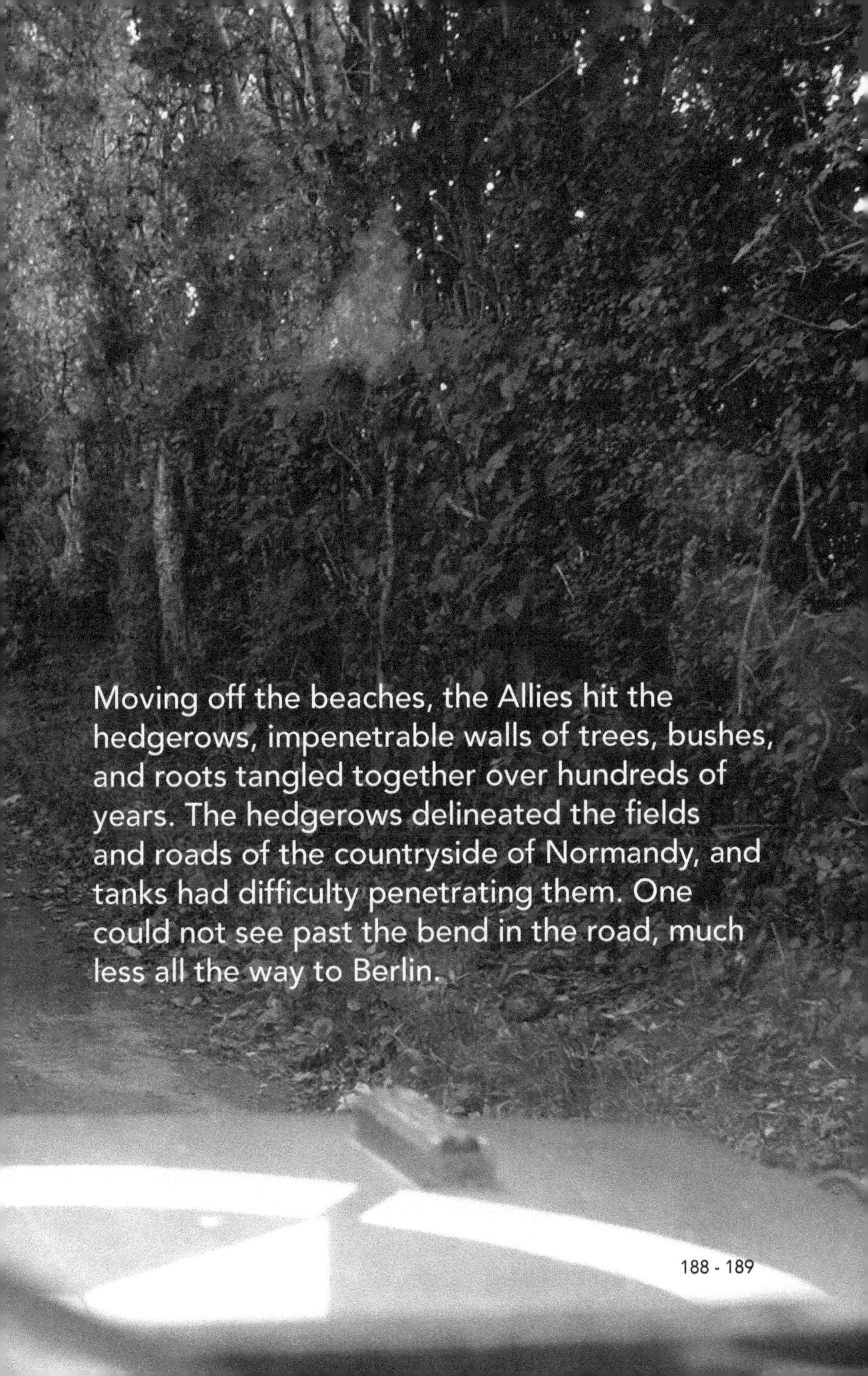

Moving off the beaches, the Allies hit the hedgerows, impenetrable walls of trees, bushes, and roots tangled together over hundreds of years. The hedgerows delineated the fields and roads of the countryside of Normandy, and tanks had difficulty penetrating them. One could not see past the bend in the road, much less all the way to Berlin.

The soldiers were forced to fight from one hedgerow to the next. By September 1944, the Allies had made it across Normandy and were headed toward the rest of Europe.

You will encounter many obstacles on your journey. Tackle them one at a time. Do not get bogged down in the enormity of your task.

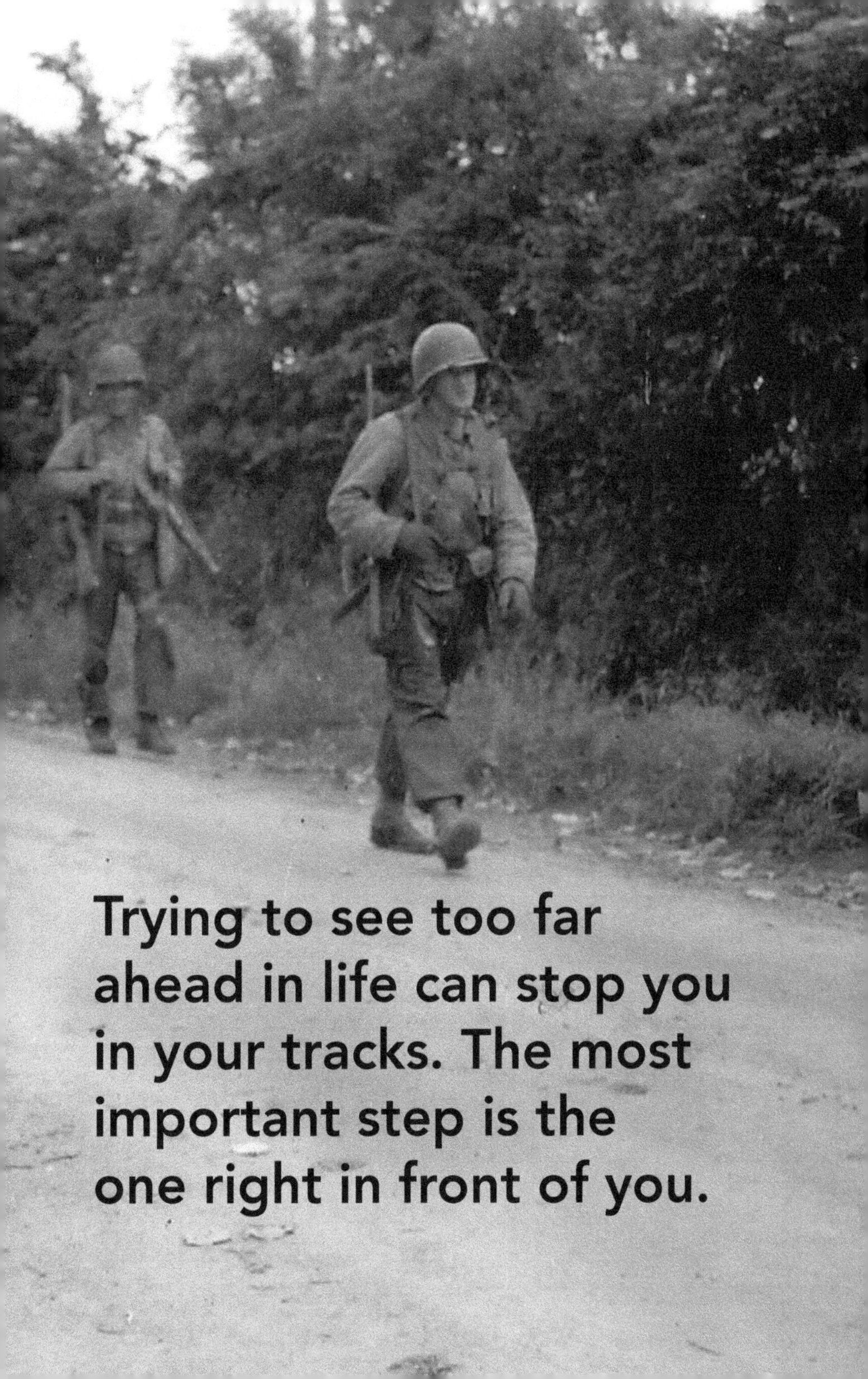
Trying to see too far ahead in life can stop you in your tracks. The most important step is the one right in front of you.

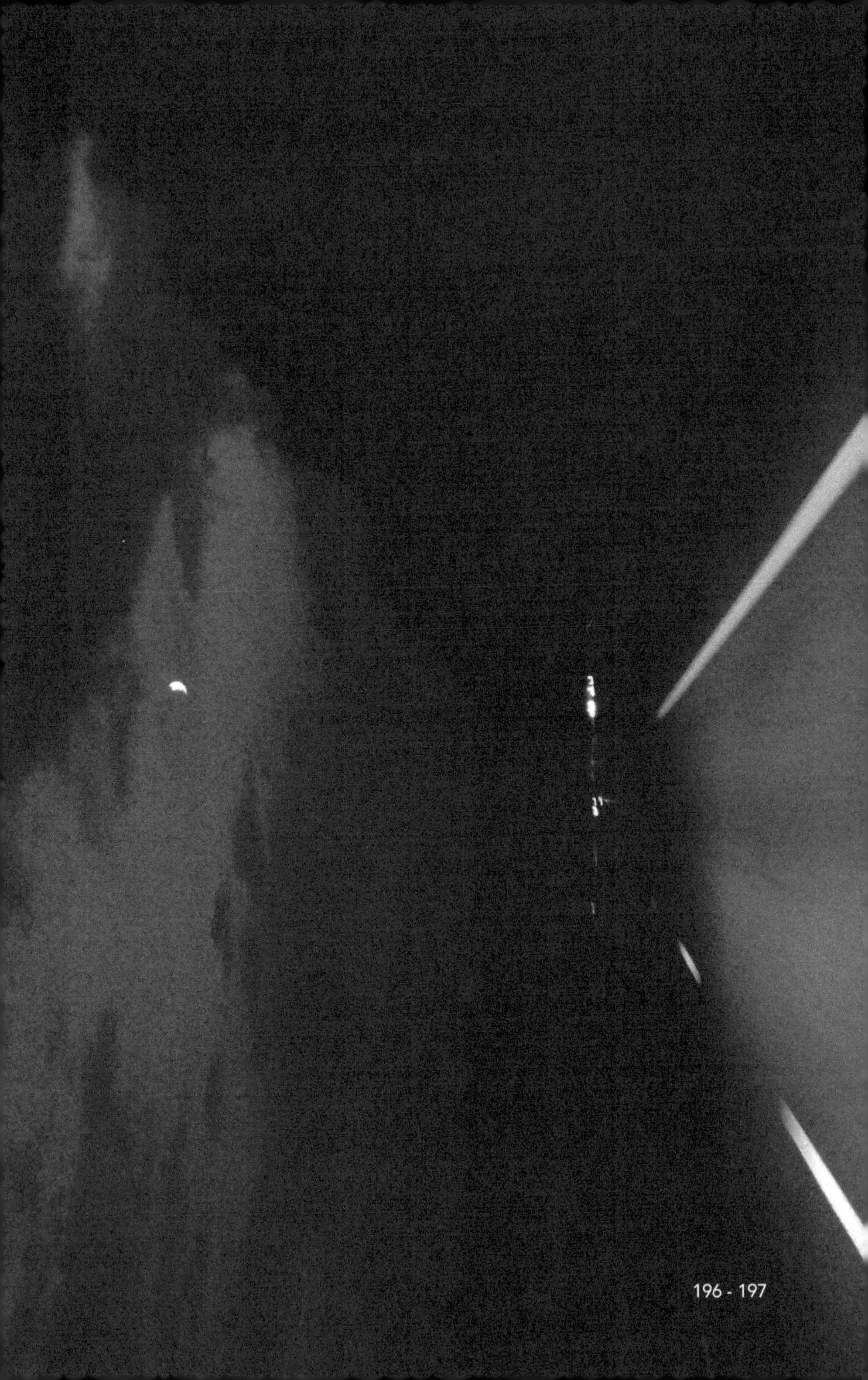

For a holiday, we often leave our house in Brussels early in the evening and drive to Normandy at night. Driving down the road in the dark, it is impossible to see all the way to our destination. We only see the road just ahead, illuminated by our headlights. The road stretches out before us, but we must go to the edge of the light to see it. Advancing one step at a time, we eventually reach our destination.

I remind myself and my children of this when we feel overwhelmed. I could not see what this book would become when I began, but one step led to another and another and another.

It is okay to be uncertain as you make your way.
Do what you can right now.

Go to the edge of the light you can see.

How will you get to the edge of your hedge

?

9

Honor
their lives
by
living yours.

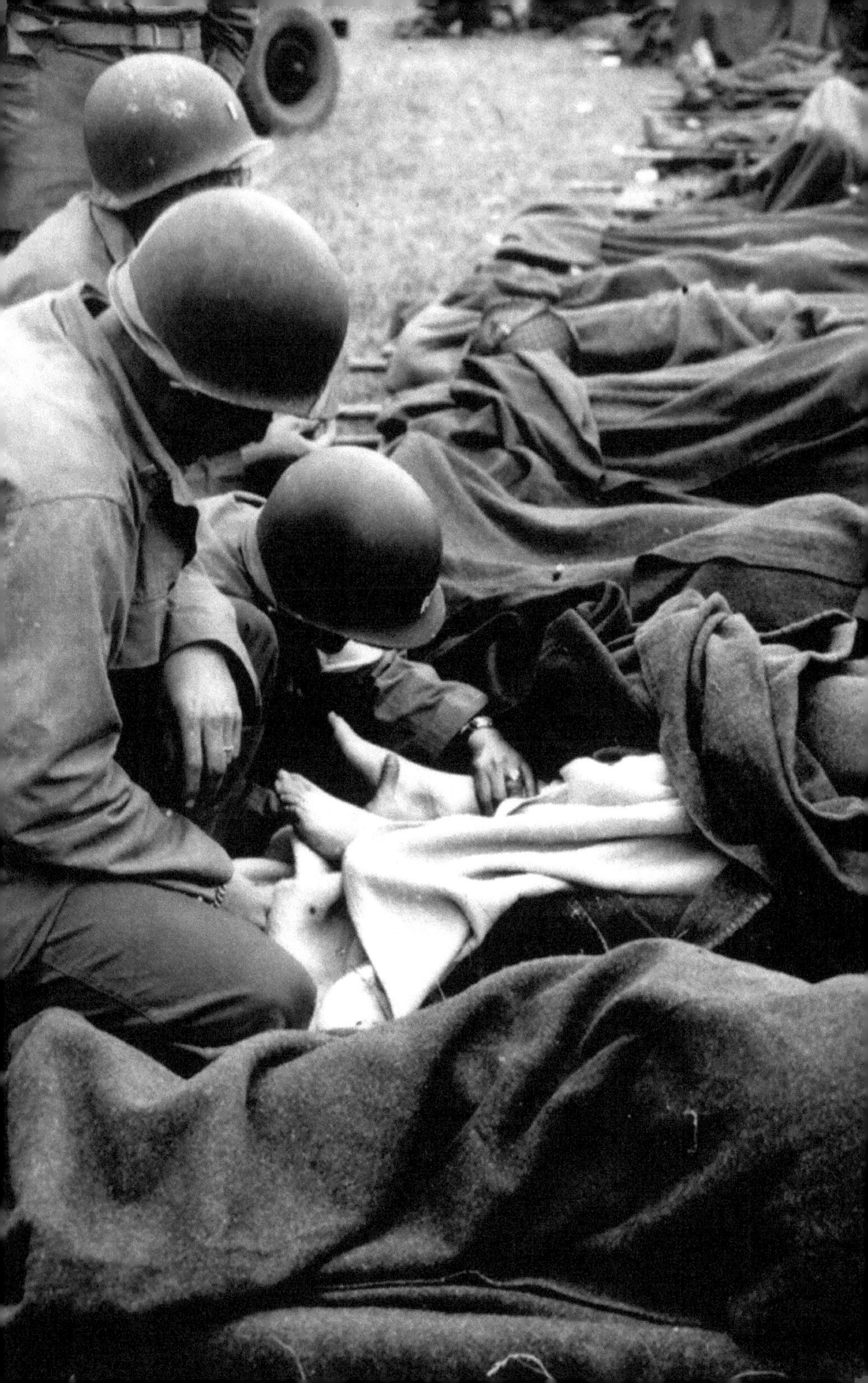

They were
soldiers and civilians,
men and women,
husbands and wives,
fathers and mothers,
sons and daughters.
Conservative estimates claim 50-80 million
individuals died during WWII.
Guilt is a common reaction.
Survivors wonder, "Why me?"
Generations that follow wonder
how to repay such a debt.

**"Death is only an incident
and not the most important one
which happens to us
in the state of being...
look forward,
feel free,
rejoice in life,
cherish the children,
guard our memory."**

SIR WINSTON CHURCHILL
writes to his wife Clementine on 17 July 1915 in a letter to be opened on the event of his death during WWI

“They gave up
all their tomorrows
for our today.”

WILLY PARR
British 6th Airborne Division

Regret death?
Celebrate life!

A family visit to the American Normandy Cemetery in Colleville-sur-Mer. Overwhelm. Guilt for a sense of debt to the fallen. Motherly guilt for dragging my children to my own place of interest despite their protests to play on the beach. A transformational shift.

"Mom, I feel strange, as if I should be dead," my son whispered. "I found a cross with my name on it." Having an uncommon name that he never finds on souvenir mugs or keychains, he was taken by surprise, and so was I. "I even found the names of each of my friends. Come."

I explained to my son that he was not supposed to be dead, but it was in part thanks to this soldier and his friends, that he could enjoy the life he does today. As we sat in silence, I realized that as a mother, I would give anything - even my life - to see my children pursue what is important to them, to pursue what brings them happiness and joy. Suddenly, I saw my parents, their parents, and generations going back in time, all wanting the same for future generations.

In that moment, my guilt vanished. I realized that the best way to teach my children how to pursue what was important to them was to do so myself. I honor the lives of the veterans by living my own.

ORLANDO VALERIO
PFC 313 INF 79 DIV
NNSYLVANIA JULY 8 194
28

It is not selfish to pursue what you love. On the contrary, you contribute to the lives of others by doing what brings you to life.

What makes you feel alive

?

10

Freedom
is not
controlling
the content
of your life.

Freedom is
creating
the context.

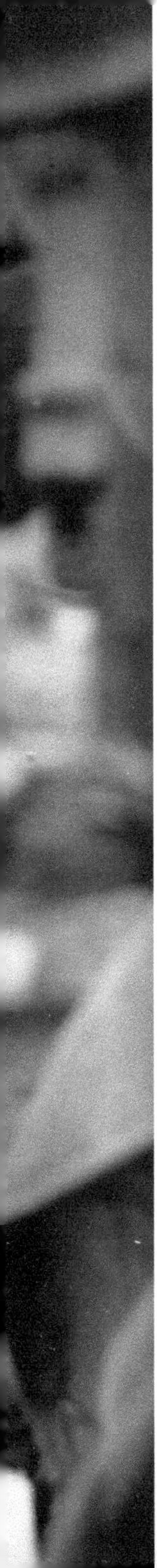

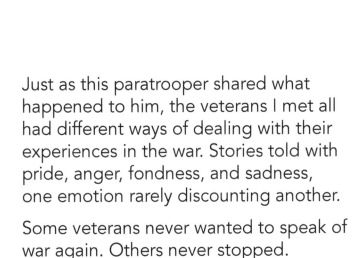

Just as this paratrooper shared what happened to him, the veterans I met all had different ways of dealing with their experiences in the war. Stories told with pride, anger, fondness, and sadness, one emotion rarely discounting another.

Some veterans never wanted to speak of war again. Others never stopped.

Observing the effect of their stories on the rest of their lives had a greater impact on me than any one specific story.

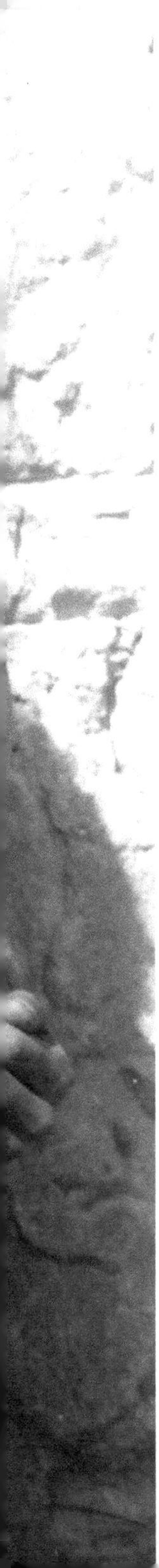

"As Odysseus, the archetypical warrior, made his way home, he narrated his journey - setting off to war, waging the long war, coming home - to listener after listener. The story grew until, finally home, he could tell the whole tale and become whole.

We tell stories
in order to live.
To stay conscious.
To connect one with another.
To understand consequences.
To keep history.
To rebuild civilization."

MAXINE HONG KINGSTON
Veterans of War, Veterans of Peace

It's not always easy to look back. Some people rush through life, preferring to leave the events of the past abandoned and forgotten like a pile of bricks.

We have all done things we are proud of
and others we are not.
There are victims and perpetrators on
every side of the story.
There are multiple perspectives
to each event.

192785

Sometimes life comes crumbling down around us, and we must pick our way through the rubble. Facts, like bricks, cannot be denied or discarded. Acknowledging and learning from the pieces of our past enables us to carry the story differently. This heals our lineage and lays the brickwork upon which our future can be built.

In this Berlin monument to the books burned by Nazis, I mourn the stories that were lost but have hope for the stories still to be written.

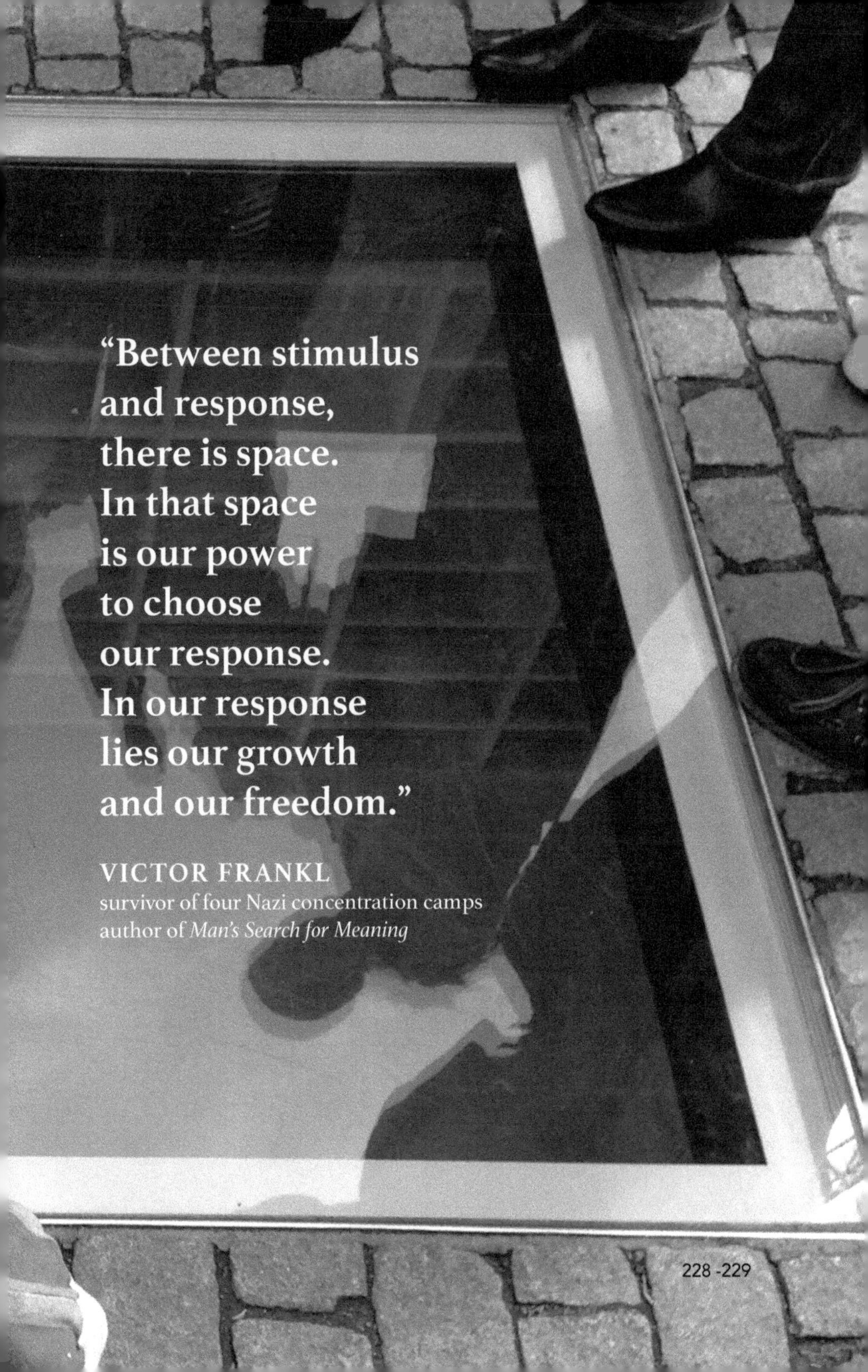

"Between stimulus
and response,
there is space.
In that space
is our power
to choose
our response.
In our response
lies our growth
and our freedom."

VICTOR FRANKL
survivor of four Nazi concentration camps
author of *Man's Search for Meaning*

Your story is not what happens to you, but what you make of what happens.

We dream, we plan, we build and then life comes along and turns it all upside down. There are forces we can influence, and others over which we have absolutely no control. Sometimes, all we can do is ride out the wave and try to keep our head above water.

In what kind of world am I raising my children?
How will they thrive in their environment?
How will their jobs fulfill them?
How will they contribute to the lives of others?

I cannot control what life will bring to my children, so I focus on preparing them to deal with the unexpected; to solve problems creatively; to look at an issue from multiple perspectives. Most importantly, I try to teach them to recognize that we each wield our own pen.

You are the author of your story.

What will you create with the content of your life

?

Does a story ever really

END...

...or just arrive at a new

BEGINNING?

D-Day is often cited by Western Allies as the beginning of the end of WWII. Hitler could not sustain fighting on both the Eastern and Western fronts. Slowly but surely, the Allies squeezed Germany until they met on the Elbe River on April 25, 1945. This iconic photograph documents the meeting of the American and Soviet armies. Cultures based on different ideologies joined together against a common enemy. Strong allies were the key to success. No one force could have won the war alone.

On May 8, 1945, Germany officially surrendered to the Allied Forces. In early August, the United States dropped two atomic bombs on the Japanese cities of Hiroshima and Nagasaki. Japan signed an unconditional surrender on September 2, 1945.

After six years and an estimated 50-80 million dead, World War II came to an end.

In 1945, the Allies began liberating Nazi concentration camps. The atrocities of Hitler's Final Solution were exposed for the world to see. An estimated 11-15 million Jews, Roma, homosexuals, handicapped, and political opponents were stripped of everything they loved, including the symbols of their love for each other, and then systematically executed.

GENERAL EISENHOWER wrote the following after his visit to Ohrdruf camp,

"The visual evidence and the verbal testimony of starvation, cruelty, and bestiality were so overpowering as to leave me a bit sick...I made the visit deliberately, in order to be in a position to give first-hand evidence of these things if ever, in the future, there develops a tendency to charge these allegations merely to 'propaganda.'"

Debates continue today as to how much was known about the extermination camps before liberation and why the Allies did not intervene earlier. Others try to deny the Holocaust ever happened.

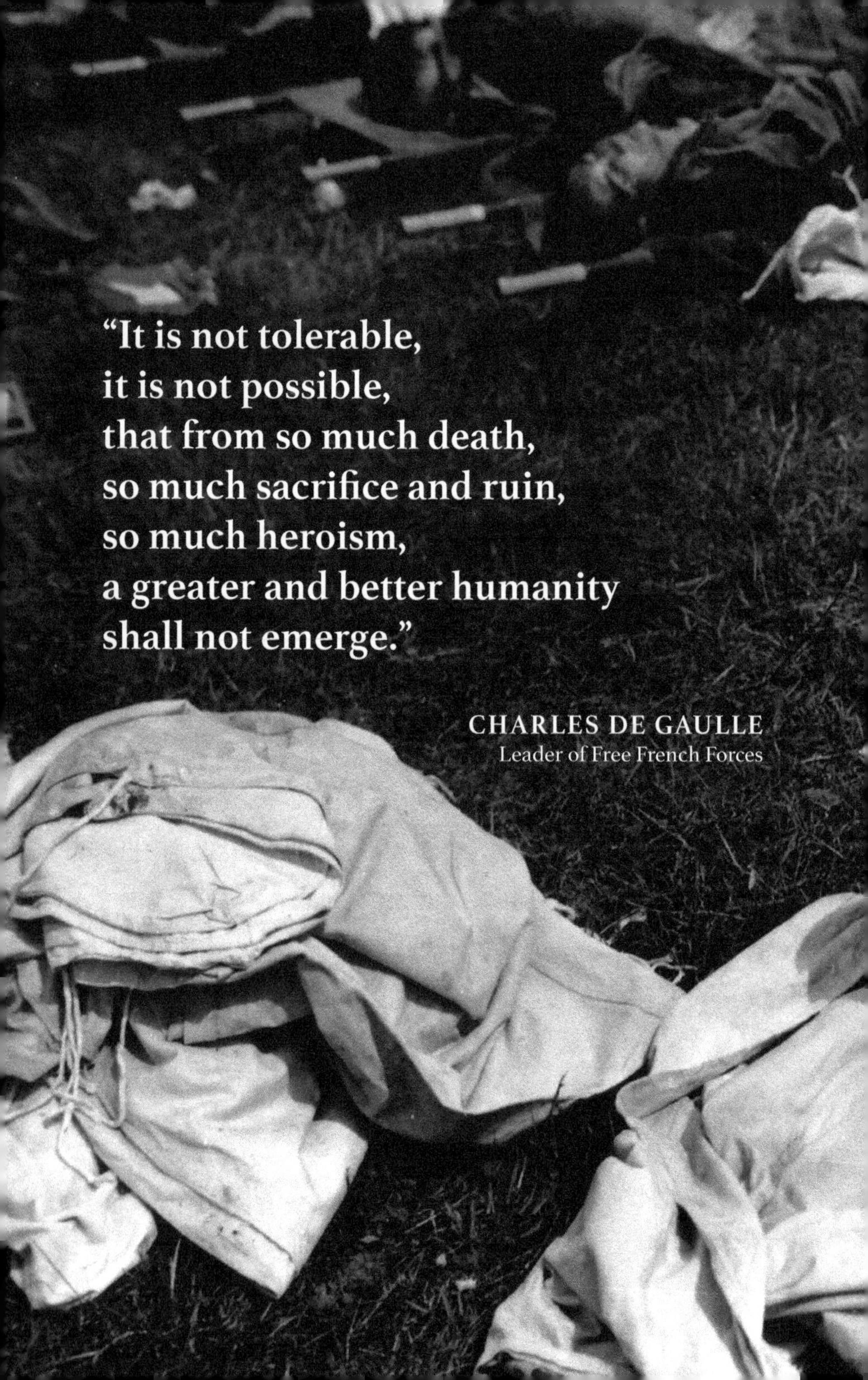

"It is not tolerable,
it is not possible,
that from so much death,
so much sacrifice and ruin,
so much heroism,
a greater and better humanity
shall not emerge."

CHARLES DE GAULLE
Leader of Free French Forces

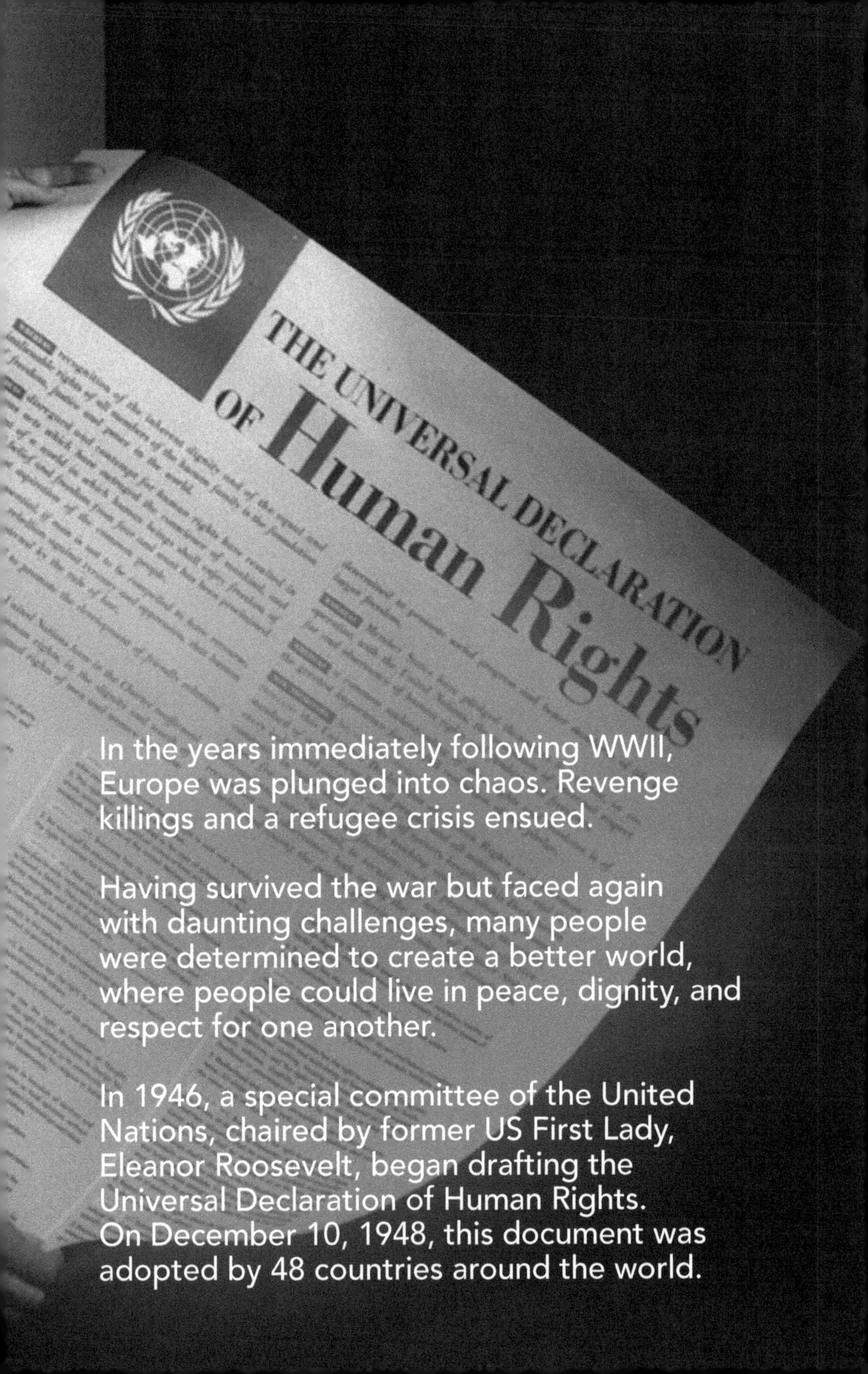

In the years immediately following WWII, Europe was plunged into chaos. Revenge killings and a refugee crisis ensued.

Having survived the war but faced again with daunting challenges, many people were determined to create a better world, where people could live in peace, dignity, and respect for one another.

In 1946, a special committee of the United Nations, chaired by former US First Lady, Eleanor Roosevelt, began drafting the Universal Declaration of Human Rights. On December 10, 1948, this document was adopted by 48 countries around the world.

War still exists today, but so does an unprecedented exchange of people and knowledge across cultures and borders.

People writing a different story.

People learning history from multiple perspectives and recognizing our common humanity.

People making linguistic, cultural, and religious walls obsolete.

People creating a future history which upholds intercultural dialogue, respect for differences, tolerance, and understanding.

“If civilization is to survive, we must cultivate the science of human relationships: the ability of all peoples, of all kinds, to live together, in the same world, at peace.”

FRANKLIN D. ROOSEVELT
US President

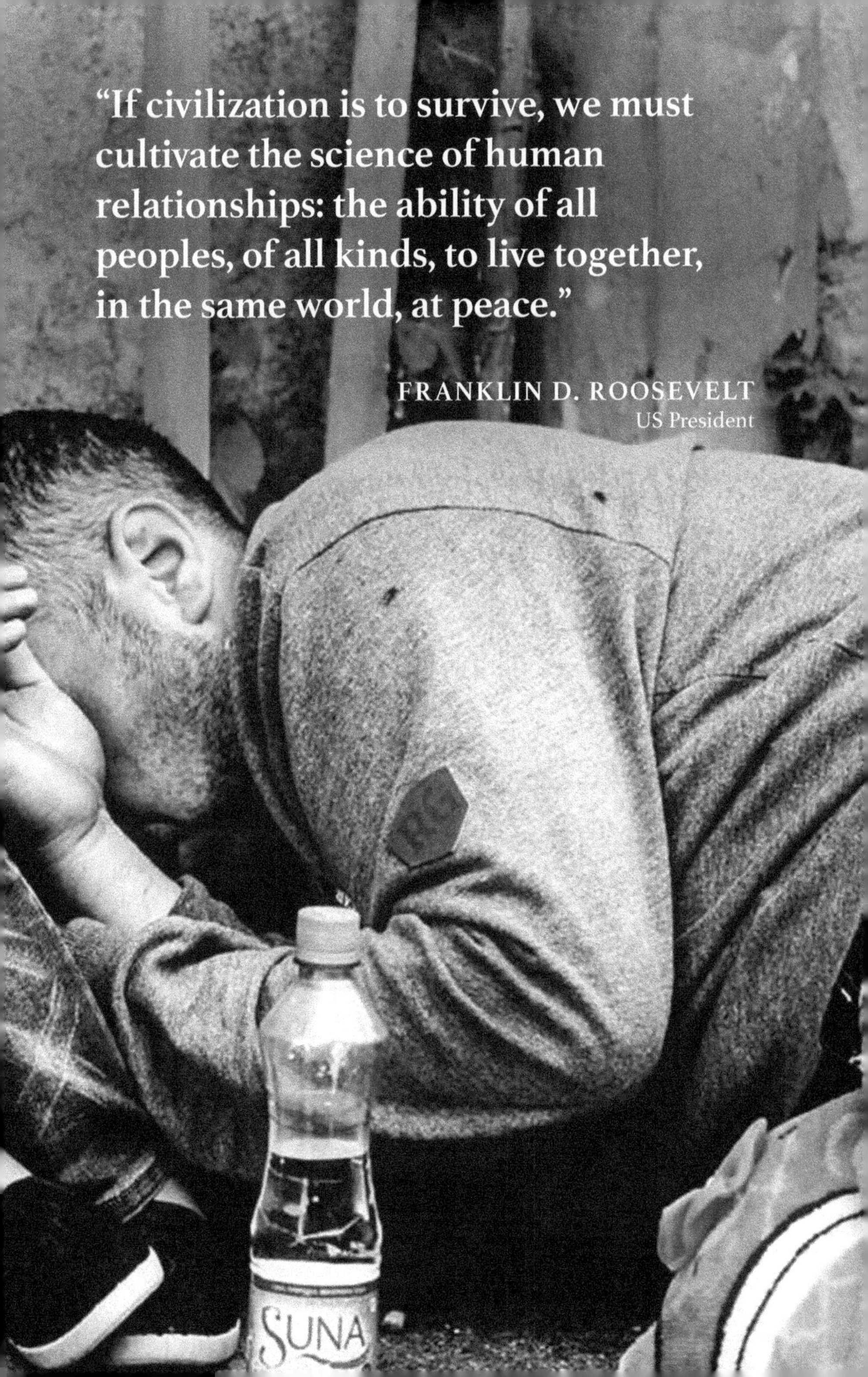

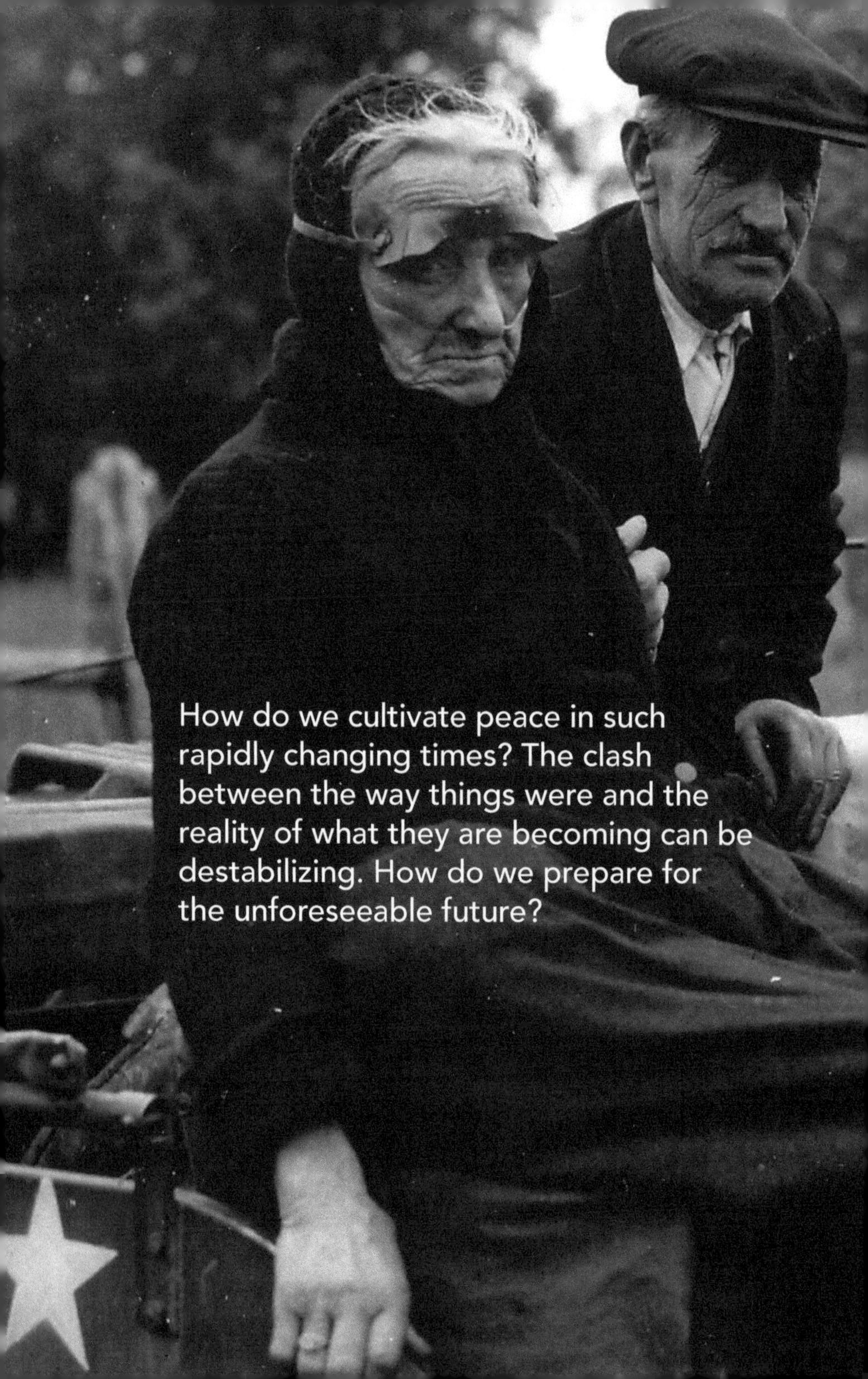

How do we cultivate peace in such rapidly changing times? The clash between the way things were and the reality of what they are becoming can be destabilizing. How do we prepare for the unforeseeable future?

U.S. ARMY

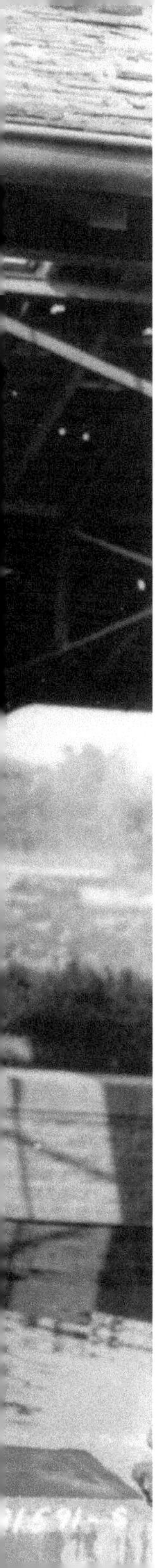

How can we maintain
our basic needs?

How can we
celebrate life
amidst chaos?

In uncertain times,
they were certain of what they stood for.
With no guarantee of success,
they moved forward.

They did the impossible by thinking creatively, inventing the tools they needed, embracing the belief that the personal leadership of each individual could make a difference, and making conscious choices each day to create their response.

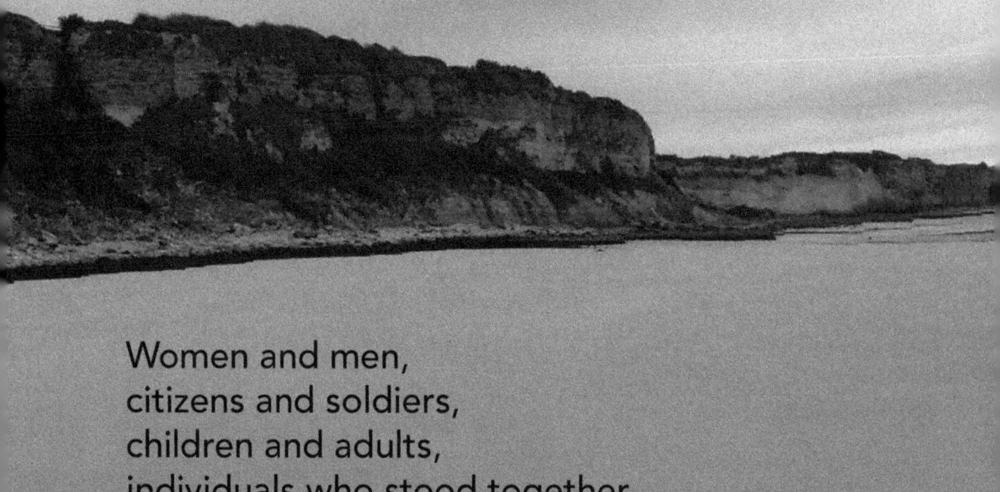

Women and men,
citizens and soldiers,
children and adults,
individuals who stood together
in the name of humanity.

They stood on the beachhead.
Navigated the shifting sands.
Took that leap.
Wrote history.

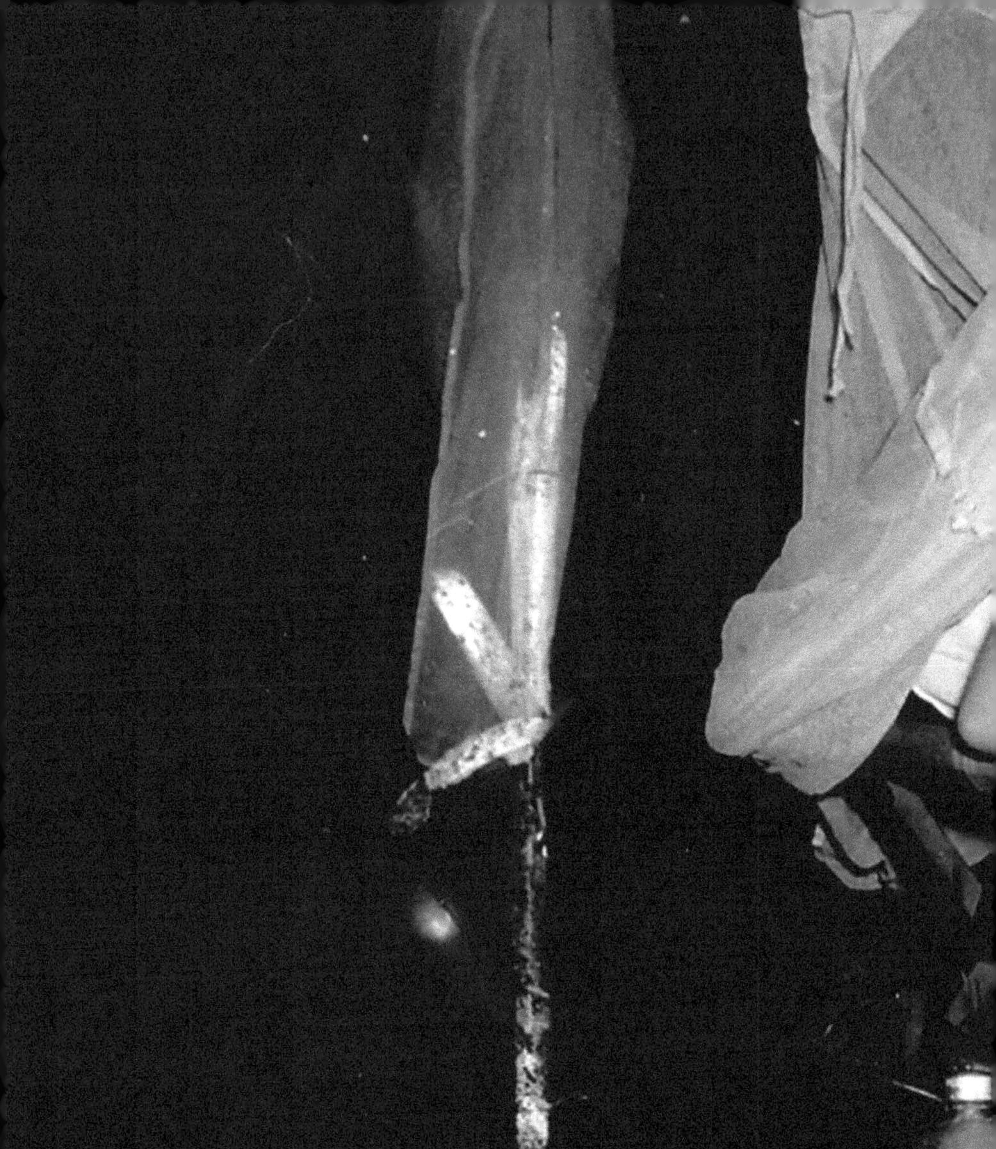

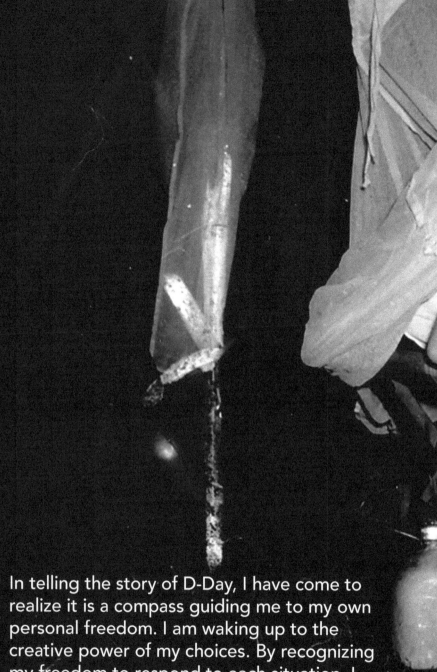

In telling the story of D-Day, I have come to realize it is a compass guiding me to my own personal freedom. I am waking up to the creative power of my choices. By recognizing my freedom to respond to each situation, I create the story of my life and the future history from which my children will learn.

Your present
is your
future history
in the making.

You create your story through presence.

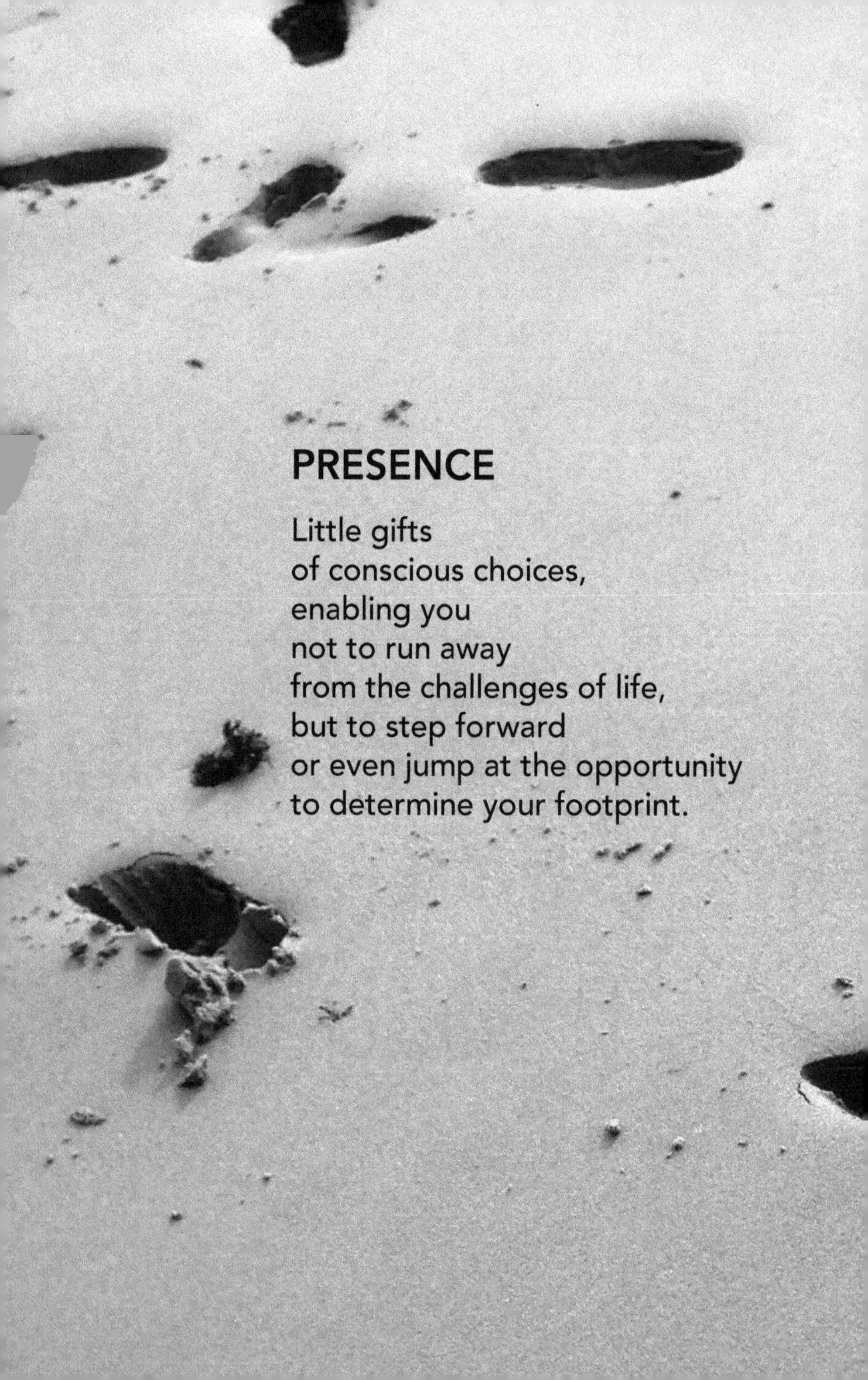

PRESENCE

Little gifts
of conscious choices,
enabling you
not to run away
from the challenges of life,
but to step forward
or even jump at the opportunity
to determine your footprint.

Your story is not written with the answers.

It is created through the questions.

1. What is your current version of "impossible?"

2. What do you stand for?

3. How can you use existing resources in new, unexpected ways?

4. What happens when you replace "Can I" with "How can I?"

5. Where are you today?

6. Who are your allies?

7. What feedback can you take from your "failures?"

8. How will you get to the edge of the hedge?

9. What makes you feel alive?

10. What will you create with the content of your life?

As we play in the shifting sands of
Omaha Beach, the Normandy American
Cemetery rests on the cliffs above us

The horizon beckons us to
stretch wider, see further, soar higher.
Rows of white crosses stand tall,
supporting us from behind.

What stories
do you want
to look back on
when you are older?

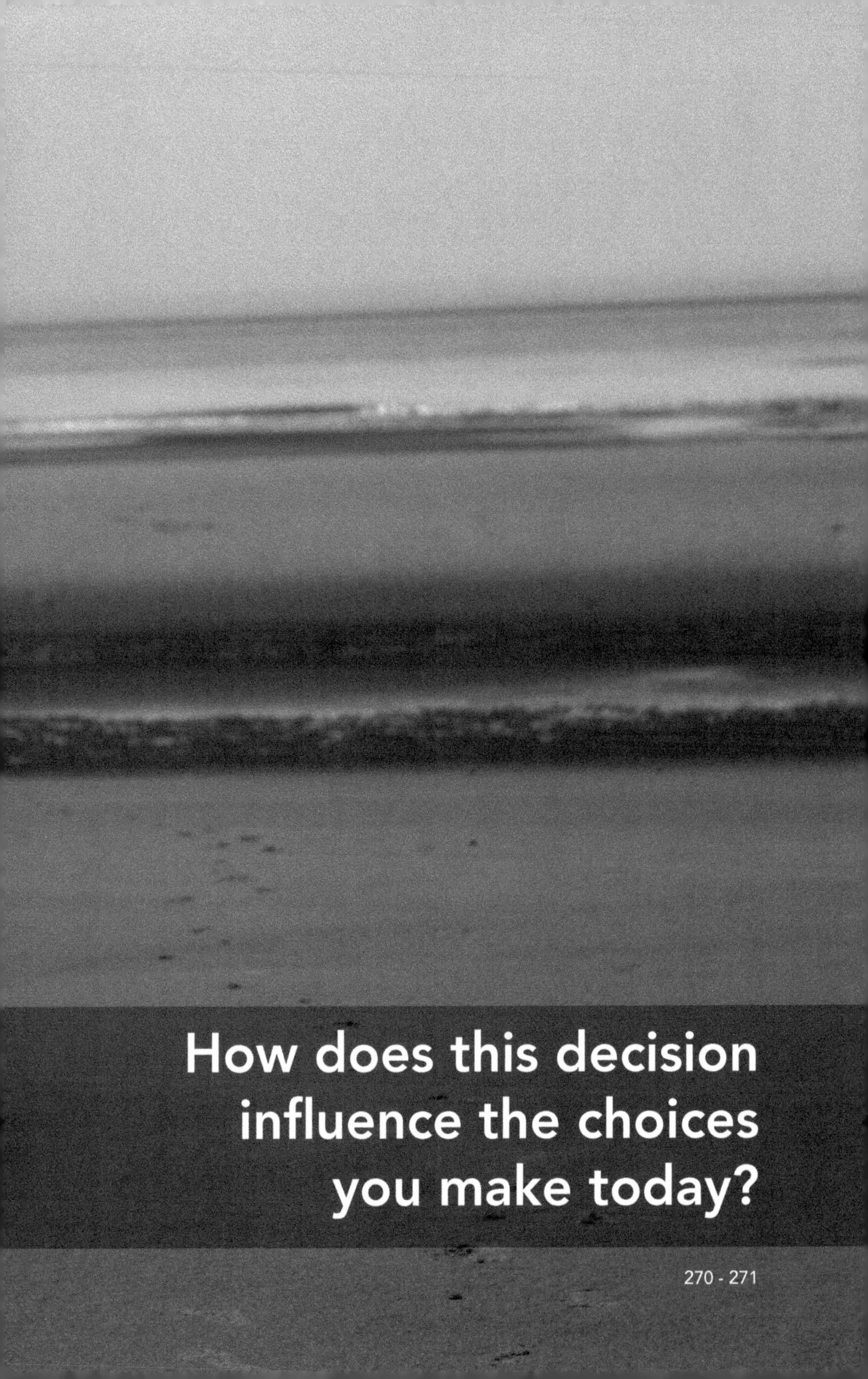

How does this decision influence the choices you make today?

Don't just
react to life.

Create your
response.

Therein lies
your freedom.

Therein lies
your future history.

Fearless Baby

PHOTO CREDITS

This book would not exist without the invaluable support of Patrick Peccatte and the photo collection PhotosNormandie on Flickr. All photos are copyright free from Conseil Régional de Basse-Normandie / United States of American National Archives - projet PhotosNormandie, www.flickr.com, except for the following:

Cover image: Children watching training manoeuvres on Blackpool Sands, Devon, UK. Spring 1944. USA National Archives.
10-11: ©Erin Meyer Charneux. Author's son at 70th Anniversary of D-Day on Utah Beach, France.
18-19: ©Erin Meyer Charneux. Author and veterans in Pennsylvania, USA, 1995.
20-21: ©Erin Meyer Charneux. The Today Show, 5 June 1994 with Katie Couric, guests Lamar Alexander & Erin Meyer Charneux.
22-23: ©Erin Meyer Charneux. Author's family in Arromanches-les-Bains, France.
26-27: Bundesarchiv, Bild 183-1982-1130-502, "Nazi Party rally at Zepenlinfeld, Nuremberg, Germany. 8 Sept 1936, the structure was designed by Albert Speer."
30-31: By historicair 23:45, 29 July 2007 (UTC) - Own work, CC BY-SA 3.0, https://commons.wikimedia.org/w/index.php?curid=2483318
32-33:By Unknown (Franz Konrad confessed to taking some of the photographs, the rest was probably taken by photographers from Propaganda Kompanie nr 689.[4][5]) - en:Image:Warsaw-Ghetto-Josef-Bloesche-HRedit.jpg uploaded by United States Holocaust Museum. This is a retouched picture, which means that it has been digitally altered from its original version. Modifications: Restored version of Image:Stroop Report - Warsaw Ghetto Uprising 06.jpg with artifacts and scratches removed, levels adjusted, and image sharpened.., Public Domain, https://commons.wikimedia.org/w/index.php?curid=17223940
36-37: By Original Author: User:San Jose Derivative Author: User:ArmadniGeneral [GFDL (http://www.gnu.org/copyleft/fdl.html) or CC-BY-SA-3.0 (http://creativecommons.org/licenses/by-sa/3.0/)], via Wikimedia Commons
38-39: "Beach Defenses, France. Hedgehogs. Note horse on beach with working party." From the Robert O. Bare Collection (COLL/150) at the Marine Corps Archives and Special Collections.
44-45: ©Erin Meyer Charneux original map created with ©mapchart.net.
52-53: Leslie Ragan. Harry Mayerovitch. Library and Archives Canada, C-115722.
54-55: ©Erin Meyer Charneux. 70th Anniversary of D-Day on Utah Beach, France.
64-65: By Anon. (Bayeux Tapestry) [Public domain], via Wikimedia Commons
74-75: ©Erin Meyer Charneux. Omaha Beach in Normandy, France.
94-95: ©Erin Meyer Charneux. Author's daughter in her mom's boots. Brussels, Belgium.
112-113: ©Olivia Charneux. Omaha Beach in Normandy, France.
118-119: https://www.flickr.com/photos/christopherbrown/10732063296/in/faves-14796008@N07/
124-125: Image of Mulberry Harbor B at Arromanches, September 1944. By Harrison (Sgt), No 5 Army Film & Photographic Unit [Public domain], via Wikimedia Commons. (Collection of Imperial War Museum, London)
128-129: https://www.flickr.com/photos/ludovicmauduit/14153490798/in/faves-14796008@N07/
132-133: ©Erin Meyer Charneux. Author's mother and daughter at Angoville-au-Plain, France.
148-149: ©Erin Meyer Charneux. Utah Beach, France.
154-155: ©Didier Charneux. 70th Anniversary of D-Day in La Fiere, France.
158-159: ©Erin Meyer Charneux. Souvenir clicker from Normandy.
164-165: ©Erin Meyer Charneux. Author's daughter with WWII veteran at 70th anniversary.
170-171: Holocaust Memorial in Berlin. By Wikformi (Own work) [CC BY-SA 3.0 de (http://creativecommons.org/licenses/by-sa/3.0/de/deed.en)], via Wikimedia Commons
172-173: Bundesarchiv, Bild 1011-291-1209-26. Photo, Koll. 1 August 1942.
182-183: ©Erin Meyer Charneux. Camp Patton in Nehou, France.
188-189: ©Erin Meyer Charneux. Hedgerows near Saint-Marie-du-Mont.
196-197: ©Erin Meyer Charneux. Somewhere between Brussels and Normandy.
210-211: ©Erin Meyer Charneux. American Normandy Cemetery, Colleville-sur-Mer, France.
212-213: ©Erin Meyer Charneux. American Normandy Cemetery, Colleville-sur-Mer, France.
222-223: unknown origin. Mediatheque de Lisieux, France.
228-229: ©Erin Meyer Charneux. Author's daughter in Berlin, Germany.
232-233: ©Erin Meyer Charneux. Omaha Beach in Normandy, France.
256-257: ©Olivia Charneux. Author's children on Omaha Beach in Normandy, France.
262-263: ©Erin Meyer Charneux. Omaha Beach in Normandy, France.
268-269: ©Erin Meyer Charneux. Author's sons on Omaha Beach in Normandy, France.
270-271: ©Erin Meyer Charneux. Author's daughter on Omaha Beach in Normandy, France.
272-273: ©Erin Meyer Charneux. Author's daughter on jeep ride in Normandy, France.
Author photos by Erin Faith Allen.
Back cover: ©Olivia Charneux. Author's son playing on Omaha Beach, France.

HOW TO SAY THANK YOU...LET ME COUNT THE WAYS:

To the professors in the Frank Denius Normandy Scholar Program on WWII at The University of Texas at Austin for introducing me to the history of WWII in such a captivating way.

To the veterans of WWII and their families who opened their hearts, shared their stories, and brought history to life.

To Kelly Garramone, who saw the light in my eyes when I spoke of writing a book and kept reflecting it back at me when I'd shut my eyes.

To Austin Kleon and his book *Steal Like An Artist,* which allowed me to believe that perhaps I did have my own D-Day story to tell.

To Patrick Pecatte who created PhotosNormandie and who has been an invaluable resource throughout this process. I can't wait for us to actually meet in person!!

To my friends who supported my enthusiasm and commitment despite not understanding much of what I was doing in the early days. Neither did I!

To Dr. David Crew, history professor at the University of Texas at Austin, treasured mentor, and friend. You washed aside my fear of a 'first book' with the encouraging comment, "of course your first book will be bad, that way all the others after can be better!" With one phrase you made countless walls obsolete.

To my talented cousin, Carey Russell, filmmaker, photographer, screenwriter, and all around amazing individual. Thank you for helping me polish the final details needed to take it that one step further.

To my parents who encourage and believe in me. I honor you by trying to always do the same with my own children.

To Olivia, Orlando, Dante & Dahlia, who have grown up during this process and helped me grow, too. You are my WHY.

To Didier, without whom none of this book, nor my life, would be possible. Your open mind and heart amaze me. Your love grounds me and lets me soar. My love and gratitude overflow multiple lifetimes.

WORD WEAVER, STIRRING SPEAKER, VISUAL ARTIST, TIME TRAVELER

Weaving together degrees in WWII history and cultural anthropology with visual and spoken arts, I use the past as a portal to address today's challenges in innovation, leadership, and human rights. I speak on TV programs and stages around the world about how we create our future history through our actions today. A native Texan, I have lived over half my life in Brussels with my Belgian husband, raising our four bi-lingual and multicultural children. Brussels is my heartbeat. Normandy is my soul's sigh.

For engaging, eye-opening, inspiring keynotes, and workshops, contact me online.

WANT TO LEARN MORE ABOUT D-DAY & WWII?

There is much more about D-Day & WWII than in the scope of this book. Go to my website for favorite books, movies, cultural resources, and places to visit.

www.erinmeyercharneux.com